CLASS
OF THE
FIELD

CLASS OF THE FIELD

New Performance Ratings for Thoroughbreds

JAMES QUINN

William Morrow and Company, Inc.
New York

Library of Congress Cataloging-in-Publication Data

Quinn, James, 1943–
   Class of the field.
    1. Horse race betting.   2. Thoroughbred horse.
3. Race horses.   I. Title.
SF331.Q545 1987   798.4′01   86-28464
ISBN 0-688-06551-1

Printed in the United States of America

First Edition

1 2 3 4 5 6 7 8 9 10

BOOK DESIGN BY PATRICIA LOWY

The author would like to thank *The Daily Racing Form, Inc.* for granting written permission for its copyrighted material to be reproduced throughout this book.

Contents

CLASS
OF THE
FIELD

1

The Problem

Why do even highly experienced handicappers have so much trouble with the class factor?

The problem is pervasive and enduring. It invades major tracks, medium-class tracks, and minor tracks. It spreads from claiming races to allowance races to the stakes. Which animal is the class of the field, the best horse today? The majority of handicappers just do not know.

On an excursion to Ak-Sar-Ben, in Omaha, Nebraska, for handicapping seminars during the week of the 1985 running of the Cornhusker Handicap (Grade 2), the town was ablaze with divisive opinion regarding the relative merits of the two big stakes guns leading the field. The race had been billed loudly for a week as a match between Gate Dancer and Imp Society. Track representatives were not bashful about promoting the race as perhaps the greatest in Ak-Sar-Ben history.

Gate Dancer had whipped Imp Society by five-and-one-half lengths at Ak-Sar-Ben in the previous year's Omaha Gold Cup (Grade 3), when both horses were three, but since then Imp Society had polished off six consecutive graded stakes in New York, Maryland, and Arkansas, while Gate Dancer at four had not yet won in four starts at four in southern California. The trainers enhanced the glamour of the event: Jack Van Berg (Gate Dancer) and D. Wayne Lukas (Imp Society).

In the days leading up to the big event I had listened with some interest to track handicapper Terry Wallace analyze each card for the daily customers. Strictly an entertainment for early arrivals, the track disavowing responsibility for the opinions expressed, the presentation is treated officialy nonetheless, with Wallace appearing in living color on Ak-Sar-Ben's monitors and on the huge screen in a unique underground amphitheater. Dressed in coat and tie and arrayed in businesslike format, Wallace plows through the day's races in rapid-fire articulate style. It's a practiced, mannered routine, well done actually, with Wallace veering skillfully from contender to contender while accenting the pluses he notes for each, and ending by providing the inevitable first, second, and third selections for each race.

The single problem with the presentation is that more than occasionally I have heard Wallace make declarative statements about handicapping that were in my opinion factually incorrect. I'd rate several of his miscues as sophomoric.

In a preliminary nonwinners allowance race of July he preferred a four-year-old to a three-year-old because of age. In fact, three-year-olds easily win more than their fair share of these allowances and should be strongly preferred by handicappers. I also thought he was wrong in overstating the probable effects of recent form. In contemporary handicapping, recent form is less decisive than ever. And I was convinced he misinterpreted the influences of high weight and weight shifts; the latter seems to me a silly uneducated mistake that has become a tiresome cliché passed around among unread, out-of-date handicappers.

Not once did I hear Wallace point out that a terrific track bias favoring closers had been stopping frontrunners cold in Ak-Sar-Ben's upper stretch all week, while propelling latecomers from far behind to upset victories.

My feeling was that Ak-Sar-Ben's customers were more misguided than disabused. Unfortunately, the practical consequence is the same, the encouragement and reinforcement of

ill-informed thinking and betting among racing's regular customers. Racetracks share a deep responsibility for this enduring condition, a worthy topic, but for another time.

In analyzing the Cornhusker Handicap, Wallace picked Imp
Society to win, a pick that I think could be made only by some-
one who failed to comprehend the fundamental principles of
thoroughbred class evaluation.

Following on page 14 are the records of the two main
contestants on Ak-Sar-Ben's biggest day.

The 1985 Cornhusker was not a match race in the slightest,
with Gate Dancer obviously the far superior horse.

Anyone who does not comprehend that should retreat to
square one in the past performances and examine the grade
designations of the stakes races the two horses have exited.
Those having access to result charts might entertain the corresponding purse values as well.

Gate Dancer's lines are Grade 1 outstanding. Imp Society's
are Grade 2 and Grade 3 almost exclusively.

When trainer Lukas attempted to sneak his ultra-sharp
Grade 2 star into a legitimate Grade 1 war, Belmont Park's
prestigious Metropolitan Mile, on May 27, look what happened
to it.

Now entertain the indisputable result when Gate Dancer entered the single Grade 3 race in its record, on August 4, 1984.

To be sure, to make use of this information handicappers
must know how to interpret the gradings of stakes. To do that,
they must first understand the modern stakes hierarchy in
major racing.

The hierarchy is not altogether complex, notably not in this
case. As a rule, rather firm, Grade 1 horses are decidedly superior to Grade 2 and Grade 3 horses. It is not a close situation. A
Gate Dancer short of peak condition can pickle an Imp Society
at its best, as trainer Van Berg gently intimated in a prerace
television interview. The rating method I shall present in this
book favors Gate Dancer by as many as 16 points.

So the discussion will not seem academic, Gate Dancer fig-
uring to go postward at miserly odds regardless, let's pursue
the handicapping of the 1985 Cornhusker Handicap to its

9th Ak-Sar-Ben

1 1/8 MILES
AK-SAR-BEN

1 ⅛ MILES. (1.47⅘) 12th Running CORNHUSKER HANDICAP STAKES (Grade II). Purse $150,000 (Guaranteed) (plus $20,000 Breeders' Cup Premium Awards, plus $8,000 from NTBDF). By subscription of $150 each, which shall accompany the nomination, $750 to pass the entry box, an additional $750 to start, with $90,000 guaranteed to the winner, $30,000 to second, $16,500 to third, $9,000 to fourth and $4,500 to fifth. Starters to be named through the entry box by the usual time of closing. (Plus $20,000 Breeders' Cup Premium Awards to be divided 54%, 27% and 9% to the owner of first, second and third horses provided they are nominated to the Breeders' Cup). The unique Cornhusker Trophy will be presented to the winning owner. High weights preferred. The field will be limited to the number of stalls in the starting gate. Horses not drawing a starting position in the gate will receive a refund of the entry fee. (Closed with 18 nominations.)

Imp Society Ch. c. 4, by Barrera—Trotta Sue, by Promised Land
Own.—Heslop Stable 126 Br.—Jones B C (Ky) 1985 10 7 2 0 $654,853
Tr.—Lukas D Wayne 1984 14 6 1 0 $136,570
Lifetime 24 13 3 0 $791,423 Turf 1 0 0 0

6Jly85-9Aks 1$\frac{1}{16}$:47 1:10^4 1:43 ft *1-3 126 2^3 2^2 2^1 $1^{1\frac{1}{2}}$ Baze RA^4 B Of Gov H 88-24 Imp Society, Set Free, SplendidTab 6
6Jly85—Grade III
7Jun85-8Bel 1⅛:46^1 1:10^1 1:48 ft 2½ 125 $5^{3\frac{1}{2}}$ $7^{3\frac{1}{2}}$ 3^2 $2^{3\frac{1}{2}}$ Day P^1 N'sau Cty H 83-19 ScrtPrinc, ImpSocty, BoundngBsqu 10
7Jun85—Grade II
27May85-8Bel 1 :45^4 1:10^1 1:34^{2}ft 11 126 $1^{\frac{1}{2}}$ 2^{hd} 6^5 $6^{14\frac{1}{2}}$ BileyJD^2 Metropltn H 78-15 ForzndoII, MoException, TrckBrron 8
27May85—Grade I
19Apr85-9OP 1⅛:46^2 1:10^1 1:48^{2}ft *4-5 125 4^2 4^2 2^{hd} $1^{\frac{1}{2}}$ Day P^6 Oaklawn H 92-17 ImpSocity, StrngthInUnity, PinCrcl 11
19Apr85—Grade II
6Apr85-9OP 1$\frac{1}{16}$:45^4 1:10^1 1:42^{3}ft *1-2 126 $3^{3\frac{1}{2}}$ $4^{1\frac{1}{2}}$ $3^{1\frac{1}{2}}$ $1^{1\frac{1}{2}}$ Day P^7 Razorback H 88-18 ImpScty, Intrspctv, StrngthInUnty 10
6Apr85—Grade II
16Mar85-9Pim 1¼:47^3 1:37^3 2:03 ft *3-5 125 2^{hd} 1^1 $1^{1\frac{1}{2}}$ $1^{2\frac{1}{2}}$ Day P^5 J Cmpbell H 106-15 Imp Society, Moro, Light Spirits 9
16Mar85—Grade III; Brushed; clear
3Mar85-8Aqu 1⅛ ⊡:48 1:12^2 1:50^{1}ft *3-2 123 $2^{\frac{1}{2}}$ 1^{hd} 2^{hd} $1^{1\frac{3}{4}}$ VelsquzJ^3 Grey Lag H 91-17 Imp Society, Verbarctic, Moro 5
3Mar85—Grade III
16Feb85-8Aqu 1⅛ ⊡:49^1 1:13^2 1:53 ft *3-5 119 $2^{1\frac{1}{2}}$ 2^{hd} 1^{hd} 1no VelsquzJ^5 Stymie H 77-29 Imp Society, Verbarctic, Leroy S. 6
16Feb85—Grade III
26Jan85-8Aqu 1⅛ ⊡:47^1 1:11^3 1:50^{2}ft *8-5 117 2^2 $3^{1\frac{1}{2}}$ $1^{\frac{1}{2}}$ $1^{3\frac{3}{4}}$ VelsquzJ^4 Assault H 90-20 ImpSociety, Verbarctic, RegalHumor 8
26Jan85—Grade III
5Jan85-8Aqu 1$\frac{1}{16}$ ⊡:47^1 1:10^3 1:42^{3}ft 15 113 4^3 3^8 $3^{5\frac{1}{2}}$ 2^1 DvisRG^9 Aqueduct H 96-17 Fight Over, Imp Society, Verbarctic 9
5Jan85—Grade III; Brushed rail
● Jly 16 Aks 6f ft 1:14 b

Gate Dancer B. c. 4, by Sovereign Dancer—Sun Gate, by Bull Lea
Own.—Opstein K 126 Br.—Davis W R (Fla) 1985 4 0 0 3 $147,000
Tr.—Van Berg Jack C 1984 11 4 2 3 $1,136,525
Lifetime 19 6 4 6 $1,316,225 Turf 1 0 0 0

31Mar85-8SA 1½ ①:47^3 2:00^4 2:25^{2}fm 2 126 3^5 $6^{3\frac{1}{2}}$ $6^{3\frac{1}{2}}$ $6^{4\frac{1}{2}}$ PincyLJr^4 Sn Ls Rey 84-16 Prince True, Western, Dahar 6
31Mar85—Grade I
3Mar85-8SA 1¼:45^4 1:34^2 2:00^{3}ft *3-2 125 7^{16} $7^{8\frac{1}{2}}$ $6^{7\frac{1}{2}}$ $3^{2\frac{3}{4}}$ PincyLJr^5 S. Anita H 83-14 Lord At War, Greinton, GateDancer 7
3Mar85—Grade I; Lugged in
3Feb85-8SA 1¼:45^3 1:34^3 2:00^{1}ft 3-2 126 5^9 $3^{2\frac{1}{2}}$ 3^2 $3^{\frac{1}{2}}$ PincyLJr^2 C H Strub 87-12 Precisionist, Greinton, Gate Dancer 5
3Feb85—Grade I; Broke slowly; checked, altered course at 1/8
19Jan85-8SA 1⅛:47 1:10^3 1:47^{2}ft 2 126 7^{11} $7^{7\frac{1}{2}}$ $3^{6\frac{1}{2}}$ $3^{4\frac{1}{2}}$ Day P^6 Sanfernando 88-16 Precisionist, Greinton, Gate Dancer 7
19Jan85—Grade I; Bobbled gate; Broke slowly, altered course entering stretch
10Nov84-7Hol 1¼:45^3 1:37 2:03^{2}ft 3½ 122 7^{20} 3^4 $3^{\frac{1}{2}}$ 2^{hd} †PincyLJr^6 Brdrs Cp — — WildAgain, †GateDancer, SlewO'Gold 8
10Nov84—Grade I; †Disqualified and placed third
22Sep84-10LaD 1¼:46^2 1:35 2:00^{1}ft *1 126 7^{12} 5^5 2^3 1^{hd} PincyLJr^4 Super Dby 107-04 Gate Dancer, Precisionist, BigPistol 8
22Sep84—Grade I; Grade I
4Aug84-9Aks 1⅛:45^4 1:10^2 1:47^{4}ft *1-2e 123 4^{11} $4^{3\frac{1}{2}}$ 1^3 $1^{5\frac{1}{2}}$ PncLJr^7 Omha Gld Cp 98-14 Gate Dancer, ImpSociety, WindFlyer 8
4Aug84—Grade III
9Jun84-8Bel 1½:49^2 2:02^1 2:27^{1}ft 4½ 126 $4^{2\frac{1}{2}}$ 3^2 5^8 $6^{10\frac{3}{4}}$ CordrAJr^4 Belmont 73-10 Swale, Pine Circle, Morning Bob 11
9Jun84—Grade I
Jly 24 Aks 5f ft 1:01^1 b ● Jly 9 Aks 1 ft 1:39 h ● Jly 3 Aks 5f ft :58^4 h Jun 25 Aks 5f ft 1:02^2 b

logical conclusion. Third choice in the wagering looked like this:

Eminency × 9-N+

B. h. 7, by Vaguely Noble—Minnetonka, by Chieftain
Br.—Happy Valley Farm (Fla)
Tr.—McGaughey Claude III
Happy Valley Farm   119
Lifetime 45 16 4 2 $680,253

1985	2	1	0	0	$13,382
1984	9	4	0	2	$87,718
Turf	7	0	0	0	$6,630

Handicappers who can appreciate that the Clark and River City Stakes which Eminency won last year at Churchill Downs are open but unlisted—meaning purse values usually fall below $50,000 and the competition will be similarly slack— while the Shecky Greene Handicap it lost haplessly at Arlington Park May 25 is a $50,000 listed event, will quickly recognize Eminency as eminently outgunned in Grade 2 surroundings. Jaded, its best days far behind, the seven-year-old Eminency also appeared on the track in front tendon bandages. No play.

Now examine the records of two longshots in the Cornhusker, Badwagon Harry and Ten Gold Pots.

Badwagon Harry   O—N+   114

B. g. 6, by Ole Bob Bowers—Mah Check, by Thermo
Br.—Waite Harry D (Mich)
Tr.—Gross Reid
Own.—Nagle K
Lifetime 78 15 12 12 $423,966

1985	10	2	0	3	$153,574
1984	23	8	2	2	$136,301
Turf	26	2	3	1	$68,009

Ten Gold Pots Dk. b. or br. h. 5, by Tentam—Pot of Gold, by Search for Gold
Own.—B K Y Stable 113 Br.—Payne L H (Ont-C) 1985 3 0 1 1 $51,931
Tr.—Rowntree Gil H 1984 10 4 0 3 $196,267
Lifetime 21 6 3 4 $314,022 Turf 8 0 1 1 $15,032
13Jly85-10Det 1⅛ :471 1:111 1:492ft 9½ 113 3nk 1hd 1hd 24 Platts R4 M Mile H 86-19 BadwgonHrry,TenGoldPots,DeJeu 10
13Jly85—Grade II
6Jly85-8GS 6f :214 :44 1:082ft 8 115 64½ 66 73½ 55¼ Platts R7 J Kilmer H 95-14 Sagittarian, Ringside,MortgageMan 8
6Jly85—In tight
25Jun85-8GS 6f :222 :452 1:092ft *6-5 115 3nk 3½ 22 35¼ Platts R5 Aw20000 89-13 ChiefSteward,Diapson,TenGoldPots 5
6Oct84-9WO 1⅜ :482 1:132 1:581ft 4 124 11 11½ 16 17¼ BcknD1 Mclaughlin H 88-23 TnGoldPots,Lundy'sLn,PrncKnsytn 5
23Sep84-9SLP 1⅛ :463 1:122 1:534sy *1-4 126 11½ 18 14 13¼ Platts R1 Alb Derby H 72-26 TnGoldPots,SkppngRock,RthsZt 11
3Sep84-9AsD 1⅛ :47 1:11 1:482ft *1-3 126 14 16 16 11¾ SthlbG7 [S]Man Derby 96-14 TnGoldPots,LordBlcony,BlzingAlrm 7
26Aug84-9FE 1⅛ (T):47 1:111 1:414fm 8¾ 117 23½ 2½ 22 32½ SthlbmG5 Intrnatnl H 99 — Axe T. V., Hurontario, TenGoldPots 8
26Aug84—Grade III-C
22Jly84-7WO 1¼ :471 1:372 2:034ft 3e 126 2hd 1hd 33½ 33¾ SthlbG7 [S]Queens Plte 83-11 KyTothMoon,Lt'sGoBl,TnGoldPts 14
22Jly84—Grade I-C
7Jly84-7WO 1⅛ :482 1:132 1:54 gd 4½ 126 2½ 2hd 11½ 1½ SthlbG4 [S]Plate Trial 78-25 TenGoldPots,Dayspring,ValDansnt 10
7Jly84—Run in divisions
24Jun84-9WO 1⅛ :473 1:121 1:451ft *6-5e 121 1½ 11½ 2hd 31½ SthlbmG5 Marine 81-17 KyTothMoon,Lt'sGoBl,TnGoldPts 10
24Jun84—Grade III-C
Jly 12 Det 3f ft :37 b Jly 2 GS 7f ft 1:23 b ●Jun 19 WO 5f ft :58 h ●Jun 13 WO 5f ft :584 h

The Michigan Mile at Detroit (Grade 2) offers $150,000—added to 3up. Badwagon Harry—the "other son" of Old Bob Bowers, incidentally—had won the Grade 2 race from far back impressively, appeared in winning form again after leaving unfriendly New York, and its late-running style had been favored by Ak-Sar-Ben's surface for several days.

Years ago handicapping author Steve Davidowitz showed his colleagues how to make money when an authentic odds-on favorite rules out wagering in the straight pools. Davidowitz argued that in those circumstances the public's second choice and sometimes its third as well will often be overbet. No finer example can be found than Imp Society in the 1985 Cornhusker. Eminency also qualifies.

Davidowitz advised handicappers to toss out the overbet second and third choices and couple the odds-on stickout with all logical longshots in Exactas, thereby converting the straight underlay to a potential overlay in the exotic pool. It works, and it did again on this memorable day in Omaha.

Gate Dancer won easily, as Imp Society faded through the stretch. Badwagon Harry came on steadily to nail second. Gate Dancer paid $3.20 to win. The Exacta returned $36.20. A 3/5 shot is replaced by a 17/1 ticket in the combination pool.

Will the day ever arrive when unofficial but loudly opinionated racetrack handicappers will be qualified and permitted to dispense that kind of sound financial advice to racing's customers, not to mention be fully prepared to identify for the good folks who flock to the races the authentic class standouts, based upon the merits of past performances that have been diligently studied and understood? It matters.

To be sure, the problem of effective class appraisal extends far beyond the doors of trackside representatives who should know better. It extends into the cliques of regular handicappers, who by and large approach handicapping as the recreational pastime or avocation that it is. These regulars are spurred in part by a profit motive and have bothered to accumulate considerable knowledge and skill at not inconsiderable

Cornhusker Handicap

NINTH RACE
Ak-Sar-Ben
JULY 27, 1985

1 ¼ MILES. (1.47¾) 12th Running CORNHUSKER HANDICAP STAKES (Grade II). Purse $150,000 (Guaranteed) (plus $20,000 Breeders' Cup Premium Awards, plus $8,000 from NTBDF). By subscription of $150 each, which shall accompany the nomination, $750 to pass the entry box, an additional $750 to start, with $90,000 guaranteed to the winner, $30,000 to second, $16,500 to third, $9,000 to fourth and $4,500 to fifth. Starters to be named through the entry box by the usual time of closing. (Plus $20,000 Breeders' Cup Premium Awards to be divided 54%, 27% and 9% to the owner of first, second and third horses provided they are nominated to the Breeders' Cup). The unique Cornhusker Trophy will be presented to the winning owner. High weights preferred. The field will be limited to the number of stalls in the starting gate. Horses not drawing a starting position in the gate will receive a refund of the entry fee. (Closed with 18 nominations.)
Total purse $178,000. Value of race $160,800; value to winner $100,800; second $30,000; third $16,500; fourth $9,000; fifth $4,500. ($8,000 reverts to BCPA; $8,000 to NTBDF; $1,200 Nom.Award.) Mutuel pool $257,327. Exacta pool $161,252.

Last Raced	Horse	Eqt.A.Wt PP St	¼	½	¾	Str	Fin	Jockey	Odds $1
31Mar85 8SA6	Gate Dancer	b 4 126 7 4	5^1	5^4	5^5	$1\frac{1}{2}$	1^2	McCarron C J	a-.60
13Jly85 10Det1	Badwagon Harry	b 6 114 5 7	6^3	6^{hd}	6^2	3^{hd}	$2^{1\frac{1}{2}}$	Lopez R D	15.60
19Jly85 8Aks1	Eminency	7 119 8 5	4^4	4^4	3^1	2^2	3^{nk}	Doocy T T	6.40
6Jly85 9Aks1	Imp Society	4 126 2 3	$3^{1\frac{1}{2}}$	3^1	4^1	4^4	4^9	Day P	2.20
19Jly85 8Aks5	Set Free	b 5 110 6 1	2^5	1^{hd}	1^{hd}	5^{hd}	5^2	Lively J	a-.60
13Jly85 10Det2	Ten Gold Pots	b 5 114 1 2	1^{hd}	2^7	2^5	6^4	$6^{\frac{3}{4}}$	Platts R	27.20
13Jly85 10Det5	Silent King	4 113 3 8	8	8	8	7^1	7^2	Franklin R J	43.10
6Jly85 9Aks3	Splendid Tab	5 113 4 6	$7\frac{1}{2}$	7^{hd}	7^{hd}	8	8	Walker B J Jr	121.20

a-Coupled: Gate Dancer and Set Free.
OFF AT 6:10. Start good. Won driving. Time, :23½, :46¾, 1:10¾, 1:36½, 1:48½ Track fast.

$2 Mutuel Prices:

1-GATE DANCER (a-entry)	3.20	3.00	2.40
6-BADWAGON HARRY		7.60	3.60
7-EMINENCY			3.00

$2 EXACTA (1-6) PAID $36.20.

B. c, by Sovereign Dancer—Sun Gate, by Bull Lea. Trainer Van Berg Jack C. Bred by Davis W R (Fla).

GATE DANCER was reserved well off of the early pace, came strongly around horses at the head of the stretch, then went well to the end under a left-handed stick. BADWAGON HARRY closed strongly but could not go with the winner. EMINENCY moved on the inside of the winner entering the stretch but could not go with him. IMP SOCIETY was never far back but lacked the required speed in the drive. SET FREE vied for the early lead then gave way in the drive. TEN GOLD POTS had good speed but flattened out in the drive. SILENT KING never made a bid. SPLENDID TAB showed little.

Owners— 1, Opstein K; 2, Nagle K; 3, Happy Valley Farm; 4, Heslop Stable; 5, Mayer Carolina & L; 6, B K Y Stable; 7, Hawksworth Farm; 8, Beebe & Harmon.

Trainers— 1, Van Berg Jack C; 2, Gross Reid; 3, McGaughey Claude III; 4, Lukas D Wayne; 5, Van Berg Jack C; 6, Rowntree Gil H; 7, Delp Gerald C; 8, Beebe Dean.

Overweight: Set Free 2 pounds; Ten Gold Pots 1; Splendid Tab 5.

expenditures of time, energy, and money. They have learned how to apply the know-how rather expertly as well to numerous intricate problems of handicapping.

Many thousands of first-rate handicappers converge today on the American racing scene. The author has benefited from casual acquaintances with many of them; has learned from several. It's been veritably a deluge, making the winning of money more difficult and painstaking than ever. A high proportion of the new-wave handicappers are extremely bright individuals—professionals, managers, and technicians. They have devoured every decent book on the pastime, have mastered the various methodologies, and virtually attack the past performances. All of them have taken up the relentless search for the edge that beats the others. In consequence, the art of handicapping has been tremendously improved just about everywhere.

The racetracks of New York and southern California are the toughest to beat, not because the races there are so competitive, but because the numerous talented players are. There are just that many more excellent handicappers at the flagship tracks. At the same time, experience continually persuades that otherwise competent handicappers can stumble badly when forced to evaluate relative class. The sudden naïveté always surprises me. I know one player so adept at modern handicapping techniques he would be clobbering the races consistently, except he struggles not very successfully with class appraisal.

The paradox of contemporary handicapping practice may be exactly that so many talented, informed, skillful handicappers should have so much difficulty evaluating class. The same daily experts who can spot a track bias as quickly as the daily double ends, can cite the most intriguing trainer patterns on any nine-race program, can vividly recall the troubled trips of losing horses, and can calculate speed figures or pace ratings requiring complex processing and multiple arithmetical adjustments too often cannot recognize the class of the field staring them smugly in the face.

Because of the failing many excellent handicappers continue

to lose. Some lose significantly more money than real abilities warrant.

Now that modern speed handicapping has been widely dispersed and the odds on figure horses have tumbled, it's safe to assert again that no one can beat this game while bungling fundamental class evaluations. Class may not be the most important factor in handicapping—no single factor is—but it is fundamentally important to every in-depth race analysis, methods notwithstanding.

In nonclaiming races, class can be counted upon to overwhelm the cheaper speed more often than not, and in the best of races at classic distances class laughs at pace. In any nonclaiming route, in fact, a most-likely-winner scenario features the class horse in sharp form and comfortably suited to the distance, footing, and probable pace. It's precisely the modern varieties of allowance and stakes races that cause so much hardship among so many competent handicappers.

The incentive to correct the imbalance is that several nonclaiming horses pay generous mutuels; and now that international racing has come to full bloom, certain kinds of well-disguised foreign horses represent the most lucrative source of class overlays in American racing. A subtle paradox characterizing the situation is that although almost all public selectors and practiced handicappers can identify the class standouts that pay little, few of them can find the class overlays.

If class is that basic and significant, why have so many modern, well-informed handicappers failed to come to grips with the subject successfully?

The answer may be as complicated as class itself, but can be disentangled as well.

A partial explanation is embedded in the contemporary practice. For the past decade the literature and practice of handicapping have moved farther afield from classical principles of race analysis and toward specialties that deal rigorously with a single factor or with a few related factors in combination. Modern methodologies that work well have displaced a reliance on the classical handicapping process.

Speed and trip handicapping have held sway since the late seventies. Early speed, track bias, body language, and trainer patterns have been used variously as key determinants of outcomes. Pace handicapping has become the latest rage. A practical imperative took control of the center. Namely, that winning handicappers today must resort to specialized information the casual racegoers do not possess and many other regulars do not use.

Unfortunately, if not unexpectedly, as more and more handicappers incorporated the modern practices, the methods became less effective and therefore less pragmatic. A back-to-basics movement in handicapping is not farfetched, as long as modern variations of the traditional ideas can carry the cause. Such movement has begun, in fact, as the popularity of high-tech methods of pace analysis attests. Pace is still pace, but velocity ratings are the modern counterparts of fractional times.

A more basic explanation of why so many handicappers misapprehend class is itself two-part.

The first is conceptual. Class has not been defined clearly enough and therefore not understood sufficiently as the multifaceted and essentially qualitative phenomenon that it surely is. In particular, operational definitions of class have concentrated on a particular aspect of the concept, specifically on those attributes that are concrete and objective and therefore more readily assessed—consistency, earnings, weight, speed, and rates of speed (pace). If operational definitions ignore or discount the less tangible aspects of class—endurance, willingness, determination, and courage—and they do, the practices that emerge from them will likely prove at least partially inadequate and disappointing.

The second explanation is historical. Traditional methods of class appraisal have emphasized either the consequences of demonstrated class—money won, average earnings, weight assignments, rates of consistency—or the quantifiable attributes exclusively—speed figures, pace ratings, claiming price comparisons, money won, and purse values.

With one exception, no method has been put forth which attempts to assess the actual abilities, qualitative and quantitative, horses have demonstrated in competition and relate those standards to new levels of competition. The exception has been my own, if you will, an understanding of past performance patterns in relation to the typical class demands of eligibility conditions.

That new approach succeeded so well precisely because it concentrated on the actual abilities of horses. The methodology was heavily analytical and evaluative, eschewing numbers and class ratings. Literally dozens of elimination and selection guidelines were provided for twenty variations of race conditions. Many handicappers reported difficulty in applying the numerous guidelines. They also experienced problems associated with storing and retrieving the guidelines and resulting class distinctions from the memory for future reference and use.

This book promotes a new method for evaluating thoroughbred class numerically. The method produces class ratings—numbers—that reflect real abilities. As class is quantitative and qualitative, the method is objective and subjective. It assesses the several attributes of class simultaneously.

Essentially, the method assigns points to the brilliance (speed) and scale ratings to the competitiveness (willingness, determination, and courage) horses have displayed at various levels of competition. A simple multiplication procedure calculates the class ratings. A few adjustments may be attached to the basic ratings. Sprints and routes are treated independently. The high-rated horse can be accepted as best in today's race; that is, the class of the field.

In my previous major treatment of the class factor, I proposed that handicappers judge horses as well suited to the class demands of eligibility conditions or not, based on extensive sets of criteria. The approach was well received by thousands of veteran handicappers, who reported they previously could not get a firm enough grip on the class factor, especially in nonclaiming races. That methodology endures as the best, most comprehensive guidance to effective class appraisal.

The rating method promoted here builds on that elaborate scheme; indeed, it is founded upon it. It borrows as well from the best advances in speed handicapping. Handicappers possessing a working knowledge of both approaches can best appreciate the new directions, a not unusual circumstance whenever change is advocated.

Even as the foundation work was greatly substantive, discounting technique in favor of analytical thought and resisting the temptation to translate into numbers abstract material that is inherently descriptive and evaluative, the new method is highly procedural. In a real sense it's offered as an arithmetical technique for implementing the broader, more substantive work more efficiently. The value of the ratings resides in their simplicity, concreteness, and ease of calculation. Without sacrificing accuracy, the ratings promise greater utility.

Beyond utility, many handicappers and most casual racegoers find their confidence bolstered when relatively sophisticated analyses and judgments can be corroborated numerically, a perfectly reasonable and pragmatic point of view. Numbers can be manipulated in clever ways to provide insights that otherwise might remain hidden or obscured. They often make plain the finer distinctions of more complex relationships. They become facile referents as well for making quick judgments and final decisions.

Numerical ratings also serve the increasingly important function in modern handicapping of record keeping. Ratings and numerical indexes facilitate historical storage and retrieval by microcomputers that complex abstract analyses do not, a not unimportant consideration in today's world of personal computers and electronic data bases. Now class ratings for every horse on the grounds can be updated and retrieved instantaneously, even as speed figures, pace ratings, dosage indexes, and other data items can.

The numbers, however, are not intended to substitute for the kind of analytical thought and practiced judgment that class evaluations are supposed to facilitate and reflect. I want to emphasize the rating method presented here is *not* a selection system. The high-rated horse is not necessarily a selection, and the highest rated horse on the card does not amount to the best bet of the day. Handicapping remains an elaborate, complicated process encompassing numerous, interrelated factors. The numbers should represent an effective technique for assessing relative class, but they do not represent the handicapping process as a whole.

As all know, the class horse loses frequently enough for all sorts of legitimate reasons, notably in claiming races. It also gets upset for dubious reasons, even when running its race. I have little doubt the book's technique for evaluating class can be reformulated into a systematic model of handicapping and studied for its efficacy in getting winners and profits, and I'm equally certain a number of creative handicappers will do precisely that, much to their greater credit and glory. But that is not my purpose. In the same way the top speed figure is not an automatic bet, neither is the highest class rating.

If these contents make effective class appraisal easier and more accessible to handicappers that consider the factor important, the book's purpose will have been achieved. The test of the method is that it should differentiate winners from losers consistently in races where the "class of the field" figures to preside on full-dress handicapping, as with Gate Dancer in the 1985 Cornhusker Handicap. A stricter test of its merits is that it should yield profits across a representative sample of races where class is known to be a decisive variable. A later chapter presents the first evidence on that point. It is persuasive.

Elaborating a systematic model of handicapping that yields consistent profits across several populations of racehorses and racetracks is far more ambitious than that, however, and beyond the scope of this book. Local handicappers must be urged once more to replicate these findings under local conditions before investing the money. They are urged further to use these contents in conjunction with other practices that continue to serve them well.

We proceed by returning to a deeper investigation of the problem posed at the top. Why do so many competent handicappers experience so many difficulties with the class factor? We might reformulate the underlying issues with two less rhetorical questions.

What is class?

What methods of class appraisal have been more or less appropriate and effective?

The next two chapters are intended to probe the answers.

2

The Conceptual Problem: Definitions

What is class?

The leading authorities have expressed their views in vastly dissimilar definitions.

Horsemen are likely as not to respond in a word; maybe guts.

Handicappers rarely mention the subject. The idle conversation between races almost never is concerned with identifying which horses might be best—unless the past performances indicate an animal is so clearly superior that everybody knows it and, facing minuscule odds, bettors wish to hear their slightly shaky opinions immediately reinforced.

Ironically, one of the best definitions ever formulated came to life fifty years ago. It was published by Robert Saunders Dowst, the leading author on handicapping in the thirties and forties. Dowst elaborated a method of beating the races which emphasized the reliability of better thoroughbreds. Dowst defined class as the ability to beat horses of a specific category consistently. Dowst went further by defining the concept of consistency operationally, and his method actually beat the races for the whole of 1936. It stopped working abruptly the next season when Dowst published the actual list of the country's most consistent horses and a grateful public bet them off the board.

Dowst's definition is out of date for modern racing. In Dowst's day approximately 8,000 thoroughbreds competed on a limited calendar. Relatively sound, fast, and fit when the season began, the horses displayed little variation in their form cycles. Dowst disregarded form entirely. Nowadays some 75,000 thoroughbreds compete on the approximately 8,000 racing days of year-round calendars. As the quantity of the competition has increased, the quality has declined. Form cycles now vary widely. Saratoga excepted, slow, misshapen horses populate the daily cards at all major tracks. Untalented, unsound, unfit, and overworked horses do not easily become consistent horses.

Probability studies have revealed that consistency is not enough to warrant a bet and inconsistency is not enough to warrant elimination. Inconsistent horses win enough. Consistent horses do not pay enough.

Most succeeding authors have concentrated on the quantitative aspects of performance to define and assess thoroughbred class. A contemporary of Dowst, Colonel E. R. Bradley popularized late speed as the key determinant and remains celebrated for his remark that any horse capable of completing the last quarter mile of a race in less than twenty-four seconds deserved a bet next out. The classiest horses were those that came home fastest. That assertion is far less valid today than a half century ago, and probability studies have revealed unmistakably that in modern racing the impressive stretch gain is overrated.

Pace pundits Ray Taulbot, Hugh Matheson, and Huey Mahl defined class as the rate of speed a horse could set and sustain. The classiest horses are held to achieve or overtake the fastest rates of speed. Handicappers are usually advised to combine the rate of speed for an early race segment with the rate of speed for a late race segment. Horses sustaining the fastest pace are the classiest.

Speed handicappers, of course, consider brilliance (speed) the hallmark of class and final time the critical indicator. The classiest horses are those capable of getting to the wire in the fastest time, regardless of what has happened early on. Speed handicappers, however, have always been careful to modify raw final times by factors they believe have influenced their accuracy.

At first the time adjustments proved inconsequential, consisting of the supposed influences of higher and lower weight, inside or outside post positions, and a magical number called a track variant, which supposedly erased all variations in running time resulting from the relative glibness or slowness of different racetrack surfaces. To the extent a specific track surface varied itself from hard to soft, as they do, and from day to day or week to week or month to month, as they do, the original track variants were more than meaningless—they were misleading.

Speed handicapping came to maturity in the 1970s when new-wave authors Andrew Beyer, Steve Davidowitz, Len Ragozin, Henry Kuck, and William L. Quirin developed adjusted final times and corresponding speed figures that had been sensitized carefully to the influences of relative class as well as the speed of track surfaces on specific days.

Class was defined still as final time, but final time in relation to competitive levels and to daily track variants.

As the sport itself tilted heavily toward speed horses—a devaluation in the quality of the competition means more and more races will be won by the cheaper speed horses, and the faster development of younger horses accentuates the role of speed in those divisions—modern speed figures have more accurately reflected the actual abilities of many horses. Speed as an expression of class has worked comparatively well in recent times. The figures represent an expedient definition of real ability that sizes up the competition of numerous races fairly well.

Soon a variety of speed-class models of handicapping began to appear. Some emphasized early speed, others late speed, and still others the rates of speed at several race intervals. We examine the most productive in the next chapter.

Forsaking speed or pace as key determinants of class, but anxious nonetheless to keep matters elementary, concrete, and objective, many practitioners and several authors have regarded a horse's earning power or its market value as the telltale clues. Thus the top claiming price at which horses have lately proved competitive defines their relative class. In non-claiming situations gross earnings or average earnings and average purse values serve a similar purpose.

The economic definitions contribute to a garden variety of comparative handicapping techniques, such that the horse that has competed most effectively against the highest priced opposition of one kind or another gets the high mark for class.

All of the above definitions suffer a serious shortcoming. Consistency, rates of speed, adjusted final times, economic indices—each deals too ambitiously with a selected aspect of what is instead a far more complicated construct, thereby understating the fullness and rich complexity of the class factor.

That does not mean that methods derived from the partial definitions will not work, perhaps powerfully, at least for a time, as modern speed and pace methods have convincingly shown. But they stand little chance of sustained success where the partial definitions do not at least refer to the actual abilities of horses or the associated methods are not elaborated in ways that honor the less tangible attributes of performance. Speed and pace definitions refer to real abilities. The handicapping activities they promote can succeed admirably or fail dismally, depending on methodology, and to some degree the types of races being dissected.

Other partial definitions of class do not deal adequately with real abilities and therefore have little hope of surviving in the arena of play. Consistency measures a horse's reliability more than its ability. Adding the notion of consistency at a specific class level helps enormously, and recent consistency has an empirical edge, but neither condition solves the conceptual problem.

Gross earnings can reflect durability or age as much as ability. Among the cream of the crop in 1986, earnings also reflect purse inflation. Before the classics of 1986 had run their course, the three-year-old Cal-bred Snow Chief had banked $2.7 million. The colt had lost the Kentucky Derby badly, had tow-roped several weak fields following abnormally slow stakes fractions, and arguably did not rank at the top of its own class.

Average earnings can reflect consistency as much as ability, and without the cushion the reference to a specific class pro-

vides. Among younger horses as well, average earnings are susceptible to the biases introduced where one or two extravagant
purses can be captured quickly. Many minor stakes of today
carry major purses. State-bred purse schedules exceed the
comparable open purses, but the horses are clearly less able.

Average purse values horses have competed effectively for
cater to the same distortions, not to mention the incessant bat-
terings those numbers have taken since the general inflation of
the seventies, the year-long calendars that escalation ushered
in, and the resulting intense competition among racing associa-
tions (racetracks) for live horses.

Moreover, even though speed and pace as basic definitions of
class deal with real and important abilities, another kind of
conceptual difficulty arises. The definitions presume the speed
referents commonly promoted—adjusted final times, fractional
times, speed figures, velocity rates—adequately reflect the
other well-known intangible aspects of class—determination,
willingness, and courage. The presumption is false, at least
much of the time.

The presumption that classy horses will be fast is far safer
than its converse. Many fast horses are none too classy. Anyone of experience will surely admit to that.

As a group, to refer to a constituency perfectly capable of
commenting on the matter from hard-boiled experience, horsemen rarely will accept fast clockings as satisfactory evidence
that they have an authentically classy competitor on their
hands, as much as the brilliance might stir their expectations.
Horsemen want to see more. Their expectations harden precisely when the rapid clockings have been recorded in
high-caliber races, where trainers can fairly presume the
horses have been more fully extended on other crucial attributes. Even if handicappers argue that horsemen generally do
not possess a sophisticated comprehension of the relations between time and class, their general reluctance to be swayed by
final times cannot be dismissed.

So while speed greatly reflects actual abilities and represents
a salient aspect of class, it remains but a thick slice of the definition we seek and is not interchangeable with the broader
concept.

Thus a conceptual problem associated with quantitative definitions of class has been partial or incomplete definition. In striving for utility, partial definition sacrifices accuracy. It's a dangerous exchange. The partial definition crumbles every time the apparently faster horse falters under pressure long before reaching the finish line. It happens all the time.

On the opposite pole of the conceptual problem have been definitions of class so broad, vague, or abstract that they surrender any claims to utility.

Stressing the complex, multifaceted, abstract nature of the beast, Tom Ainslie defined class tersely as quality of performance in competition. Bill Quirin became a bit less vague, referring to class as the ability to perform competitively against a given level of competition.

While these definitions are undeniably valid, they remain so global and inclusive that usually they are followed in exposition with playbacks of the conventional methods by which abstract global phrases like *quality of performance* and *ability to perform competitively* have been operationally transformed and by assertions that thoroughbred class is something more readily observed than defined. Both Ainslie and Quirin supply excellent discourse on the intricacies inherent in the relations between speed and class, and Quirin has brilliantly demolished the fashionable reliance on average purse values as a means of class appraisal; but neither writer supplies a definition that handicappers can actually employ to make class distinctions.

Global definitions that are essentially abstract suffer a conceptual shortcoming quite the opposite of partial definitions that are relatively concrete. The global definitions achieve a high degree of accuracy, but they sacrifice similar degrees of utility.

So the conceptual problem dogging the practice of class handicapping practically from its onset has been inadequate definition of one kind or another. Polar positions which the leading authorities have staked out have meant that whatever directions class handicappers choose to pursue they are being misled. By subscribing to the more practical positions, handicappers have suffered the consequences of partial definition. By subscribing to the more abstract positions, they have suffered the consequences of global definitions. Partial definitions are not sufficiently accurate. Global definitions are not sufficiently useful. The class of the field therefore is not sufficiently understood.

The solution is a definition of class that embraces both the practical and the abstract elements of the concept. At the same time we wish to avoid becoming cumbersome or verbose. That itself is problematic. The practitioner becomes confused.

Consider the attributes of class we intend to embrace:

1. *Class is multidimensional.* Class consists of several distinct ingredients of the same mixture, including brilliance (speed), endurance (stamina), and competitiveness (determination, willingness, and courage). Moreover, the three attributes interact; are interrelated. A complete and appropriate definition must therefore integrate the elements of speed, endurance, and competitiveness.

2. *Class encompasses components of performance both quantitative and qualitative, the concrete and the abstract.*

The presumption that the quantifiable components of a horse's performances adequately reflect the several qualities of class in combination is not tenable for numerous handicapping situations. Turf races leap to mind. In nonclaiming races only the aggressive horses progress, notwithstanding prior outings that have been fast but relatively uncompetitive. Races at classic distances rarely go to the lackluster swift.

Put plainly, numerous horses sporting relatively high figures and pace ratings are routinely pounded into submission by opponents having comparable numbers but greater competitive fire and fight. In close finishes, the more determined horses exert their deeper reserves throughout the stretch. They extend themselves to whatever degrees become necessary. Whether by a length, a neck, a head, or a nose, the more rugged types win. The numbers will look alike, but the horses are not.

In longer races, the qualities of willingness and determination complement the stayer's deeper reserves of endurance, itself a kind of intangible, often genetically transmitted. The intermingling of speed, stamina, and determination becomes far more complex. Distance performances are not as readily distilled by numbers alone, notably numbers obtained from shorter races and designed primarily to assess greater quotients of speed. When a speed figure of 87 at six furlongs is projected to 1:51 3/5 (87) for a mile and one-eighth, it might facilitate the sorting functions of handicapping, a helpful expedient procedure, but the projection may be dreadfully wrong as well.

3. *Class is dynamic.* The abilities and preference of racehorses change throughout their careers. Soundness plays a role. So does physical maturation and aging. So does competitive seasoning and training.

Relatively sound, fit, and eager three-year-olds change dramatically throughout that season. Many four-year-olds still seek their competitive niches far into that season. And horses beyond age six largely endure in various stages of unsoundness.

The common pattern of change is of deterioration and a steady decline in relative class, interrupted intermittently, when aches and pains subside for a spell and temperament improves. Claiming classes can be expected to vary widely, and do, especially during today's unending seasons. When getting fit and feeling fine again, claiming horses can soar to previous levels for a time, long after they seem to have plummeted irretrievably. Eventually, they will drop down again. Stable changes (claims) can accelerate either pattern.

So class becomes dynamic. It changes for all thoroughbreds. For certain horses it can change from race to race. For most horses it changes gradually and more predictably. As class changes, so must the corresponding figures or ratings, else class handicappers will be lost.

4. *Class is relative.* The best $25,000 claiming sprinters on the grounds cannot duplicate their feats when entered against classified allowance sprinters. Many will falter as badly against $50,000 claiming horses. Some cannot move ahead successfully to the next level. Allowance horses cannot endure against authentic stakes stars, no matter how sharp they feel. Early speedsters that are cheap stop abruptly when matched against the similar early swift of horses that are high quality.

Three-year-olds that breeze through preliminary conditions of eligibility can disappoint almost mysteriously when
confronted by multiple allowance race winners that are
progressing toward the stakes.

The pecking order among racehorses is real. Barriers between certain levels of the competition become impenetrable.

So class is relative to its opposition. It runs a true course only
against appropriate levels of competition and cannot be demonstrated nearly as well when overextended. Any adequate
definition must therefore retain a reference to changing levels
of opposition, as Dowst insisted fifty years ago.

The several attributes inherent in the concept of class un-
derscore the problems of inadequate definition so prevalent in
the literature. To be representative or inclusive, the working
definition must embrace qualities of speed, endurance, and
competitiveness in combination, encompass quantitative and
qualitative elements, reflect the highly dynamic nature of the
factor, and put all of the above in a context of changing opposition.

Definitions that are adequate might also be abstruse. To wit:
Class is the simultaneous expression of a thoroughbred's
speed, stamina, and determination, a race-specific level of performance that is highly susceptible to alteration due to changes
in soundness, age, or general fitness, and is demonstrably effective to varying degrees depending on the caliber of the opposition. That covers the bases but is a distasteful mouthful.

Perhaps an acceptable working definition can be forged by
borrowing familiar concepts from prior sources. From Dowst
we can borrow, not the concept of consistency, but that of
demonstrated ability against a specific category of horses.

From speed handicappers we can lift the concept of par
times for various class-distance categories. A performance better than par can reflect a higher order of brilliance within a
specific category. Above-par performance supplants consistent
performance.

We might invoke the progressive conditions of eligibility and
claiming-price scales to salute the relative character of class.

From the global definitions we can take the notion of a "competitive performance" to mean one that visibly expressed a

high degree of determination, willingness, or courage. The notion of a "determined" effort across specified distances or time intervals can satisfy for the broader concept.

To embrace the quality of endurance we can consider performances grouped at the same or related distances. Probability data support the proposition.

The crucial interplay between form and class, the dynamic component, demands the qualification that form remains intact.

A new working definition of class sounds like this: Class is a determined manner of performance at the same or related distances that is above-par for a specific category of opposition, provided form has remained intact.

An uncontested victory does not count as an expression of class by this definition, handicappers should note, regardless of the brilliance recorded. The competitive qualities were absent.

Breaking down the definition into its constituent parts, class refers to a

- Determined manner of performance
  (expresses clearly observable elements of determination, willingness, or courage)
- At the same or related distances
  (endurance has been taken into account, and sprints will not be interchangeable with routes)
- Above-par for a specific category of opposition
  (faster than the par time for a particular class-distance category, such that time is set relative to the caliber of the competition)
- Provided form has remained intact
  (the quality of a performance is expressed as a function of form, and the dynamic nature of true performance is retained)

In practice, the distance factor can be separated out by specifying that sprints and routes are to be evaluated independently.

Similarly, the provision on current form can be disassociated from the actual ratings. Although they have hardly been discarded, standards of winning form have been relaxed of late. Class and form are more disparate than ever. Only a decade

ago class appraisal was predicated on positive form, but the
dynamic has shifted. Now declining numbers suggest de-
teriorating form. Moreover, positive form has yielded to acceptable form. A five-furlong workout within the past fourteen
days can be considered acceptable form, and regardless of the
layoff. Positive form is now accepted as a complement or supplement to class, not its anchor. Handicappers can consider the
probable influences of form after class ratings have been assigned, not before. Treating the form factor *a priori* eliminates
too many eventual winners today.

The multi-part definition now might be represented by the
convenient formula:

$$\text{Class of the field} = \frac{\text{Brilliance}_{(x)} \times \text{Manner of Performance}_{(x)}}{\text{Level of Opposition}_{(y)}}$$

where

> *Brilliance* means speed above or below par in an actual
>   race
>
> *Manner of performance* means the degrees of determina-
>   tion observed in an actual race
>
> x refers to the race being rated
>
> *Level of Opposition* means a specific category of competi-
>   tion identified by the conditions of eligibility
>
> y refers to today's race

To condense the ideas and reduce the wordiness further, we
get a working definition represented by the formula

$$\text{Class} = \frac{\text{Speed}_{(x)} \times \text{Competitiveness}_{(x)}}{\text{Level of Difficulty}_{(y)}}$$

The crucial role of adequate definition becomes evident if
handicappers can accept the proposition that methodological
problems flow directly from conceptual problems.

That's been the plight of class handicappers, as the next
chapter tells, practically since the day the Dowst class-consistency system stopped working in 1937.

3

The Historical Problem: Methods

What methods of class appraisal have been more or less appropriate and effective?

If sound definition leads to effective method, it's little wonder the Dowst class-consistency system beat the races throughout 1936. The method of selection depended upon this simple rule:

> Play to be limited to horses which had won at least a third of their starts while finishing in the money at least half the time, provided any qualifying horse is the only one of its kind in the race.

Handicappers relied upon the information at hand in *Daily Racing Form*. Horses were rated on this year's record where ten starts showed, or last year's as well where fewer than ten races had been run. Dowst also provided ten rules of exclusion, his warnings about horses that did not qualify regardless. One of the rules forbade wagers on horses when "definitely stepped up," dramatizing Dowst's high regard for class barriers.

Paradoxically, the simplicity that contributed to the method's wide appeal also assured its demise. Suddenly the complicated game of racing could be reduced to a formula for Everyman. As Dowst was easy to understand and implement, practically all racegoers followed his advice. The odds on Dowst's consistent horses plunged through the floor, and the method stopped working.

For almost half a century no method of class handicapping even rivaled Dowst's in appeal or effectiveness. Most that managed to gain a measure of legitimacy for a time proved in the end as ineffectual as the definitions that spawned them were inappropriate.

Speed as Class

First renditions of speed handicapping proved pointedly worthless. Basic ratings were derived from unmodified final times that had been compared to the local track records for the various distances. Track time records were set equal to 100, and a point was deducted for each one-fifth of a second a horse finished slower than the standing record.

This assured that faster horses would earn higher ratings, but the equivalence and comparability of the ratings among class levels and distances were preposterous. Where the six-furlong record had been set by a speedy high-priced claiming horse, the mile mark by a Dr. Fager, and the mile and one-quarter by a Secretariat, the analytical problems begin to crystallize, not to mention the fruitless comparability of ratings obtained by horses at sister tracks on the circuit, even at the same distances.

Naturally, ordinary horses can more readily approach the time records of slower horses, notably at shorter distances, thereby earning apparently higher speed ratings. But an 83 at Track A might be five lengths faster than an 83 at Track B, the numbers notwithstanding. A veritable host of grievances arise when local track records are embraced as points of reference.

To make matters worse, the daily track variant (surface speed) was obtained by averaging the points below the track records (100) the winners on a given card could earn. The awful horses of Thursday could be expected to yield high variants while the fancier horses of Saturday would yield lower variants. No matter that Thursday's surface might have been faster than Saturday's. Those kinds of variants contribute nothing but headaches and upsets once handicappers attempt to apply them.

Finally, to insure that an inherently illogical situation might become absurd, basic speed ratings were further adjusted to account for the supposed influences of weight and post position. Weight has never been an independent factor in handicapping, and its only bearing on predicting race outcomes is now understood to be inverse to the traditional belief. That is, the high-weighted horses should be strongly preferred. Additional weight is far more positive than weight off. The original speed handicappers' adjustments behaved in opposite ways, lowering the ratings of the high weights and of horses adding pounds.

Likewise, post position has an incidental influence on race outcomes, unless temporary biases have been observed, and therefore lays no claim to basic adjustments of speed ratings.

So the original speed handicapping methods practically controverted the purposes and desirable practices of that genre. In the beginning speed handicapping was bad handicapping. It didn't work and gained a deservedly pitiable reputation in the bargain.

First attempts to repair the situation accomplished little more than a palliative. Final times were purportedly adjusted according to the relative surface speed of different racetracks.

The final times at regularly run distances were averaged and compared. From the home track's baselines, the final times of other tracks were rated faster or slower by the standard differences in their respective averages. So Bay Meadows might be rated three lengths slower than Hollywood Park, and Hollywood Park two lengths faster than Santa Anita, making Bay Meadows a tick slower than Santa Anita. The averaged differences in averaged speed ratings were called track variants, and they were added or subtracted from the raw final times recorded at the respective ovals. By this primitive procedure, all shippers were rated.

Moreover, the differences in averaged final times among the regularly run distances were noted, and these became the standards for constructing the initial speed charts. The charts embody the principle of parallel time. This suggests, for example, that horses that win at six furlongs in 1:11 at Track A will run the extra distance to a mile and one-sixteenth there in standard time, say 33 seconds, thereby finishing at 1:44 seconds. Horses that travel the six furlongs in 1:12 therefore will complete the same middle distance in 1:45.

Parallel time charts were used to compare horses at the same track when distances changed or when class and distance changed simultaneously. To state the obvious, they were not highly accurate.

Reliance on intertrack variants and parallel time charts never gained a solid footing among intelligent speed handicappers and never attracted a wide respectability. Among recreational handicappers the practices ebbed and flowed in the sixties and early seventies, but faded rapidly after that, when the authentic advances in speed handicapping came to pass.

The key advances, not unimportantly, saluted the fundamental importance of class. They were hinged absolutely to the idea that speed and class are entirely interlocking, which they are. Track time records were summarily replaced by class-distance par times, the averaged final times recorded by horses at the several class and distance levels of the local track, such as $16,000 claiming horses at seven furlongs.

Now variations from par were used to arrive at daily track variants. Speed handicappers calculated a sprint and route variant, respectively. These were applied to raw final times to produce adjusted final times. Adjusted final times were translated into speed figures.

Daily variants thus became sensitive to class levels, ruling out differences in class as the primary cause of variations in typical times. The procedure soon persuaded thousands of regular handicappers at tracks large and small that the standard deviations from par were greatly indicative of track surface speed on any given day.

Adjusted times and speed figures at last reflected both relative class and the daily speed of the track surface. To the basic figures obtained for claiming races open to older males, computer studies of thousands of races across the nation identified the standard adjustments that controlled for variations in final times due to age, sex, and time of the season.

In comparing horses at various distances, the concept of parallel time gave way to proportionate time, so that all horses switching distances were no longer expected to cover the added furlongs in the same intervals of time. Horses that ran faster at shorter distances were expected to run longer distances proportionately faster. Slower horses would go proportionately slower. Speed charts designed to reflect proportionate times more closely resembled reality.

For the first time speed figures supplied handicappers with reasonably accurate estimates of true speed. The numbers were decidedly more accurate than the raw times or unmodified ratings supplied by *Daily Racing Form.*

At the same time, speed as a decisive factor in handicapping was becoming more dominant than ever. Racing calendars were expanding tremendously. The number of racehorses needed to fill the daily national programs expanded in kind. Commercialized breeding programs proliferated, and the resulting progeny used a cheaper brand of speed as their trump. Speed figures that were much more accurate were suddenly much more meaningful. The figures represented many a final decision in handicapping, particularly in claiming races. Speed handicapping began to succeed admirably. It produced large sums for its surest practitioners.

As the seasons turned and speed handicapping became amazingly popular, the leftover problems concerned wide variations about par within each class-distance category. The $25,000 claiming horses at Local Downs might average 1:11 flat for six furlongs, but some won in 1:10 and some won in 1:12, and others won at the fifths of seconds in between. As pars among class-distance categories normally were set at one-fifth or two-fifths of a second apart, contemporary speed handicapping still allowed for numerous time overlaps within and between class levels. How to distinguish "class within a class"?

The situation can be controlled to an extent merely by examining the daily track variant and individual race variant in tandem. Note the following:

| Daily track variant | +1 |
| Race variant | +4 |

On a day when the winners went faster than par by one-fifth on average, at least one winner went faster than par by four-fifths, suggesting a superior race indeed.

Or does it?

This works satisfactorily when race variants cluster within a point or two but a single race sticks out. When race variants spread out above and below par or cluster above and below unevenly, such as slow two-three for races one through four but fast three-four for races seven, eight, and nine, the averaging of race variants might obscure real differences it is supposed to clarify. Are the extreme variants due to differences in class or has the surface speed changed dramatically?

When race variants are consistently above par by several points, perhaps on a Saturday, do those numbers represent relatively classy performances or was the track surface just extra fast that day?

In either case final times will be adjusted upward by several points as a matter of procedure. Is the adjustment an intelligent correction, or are classier performances being brought artificially into line?

Modern speed handicappers still have difficulty distinguishing among the fastest, most competitive races. However well they might have estimated true speed, the figures not only remain susceptible to gross errors of measurement, they also do not measure the intangibles well and do not necessarily reflect them. Was that extra-quick winner all-out exhausted, or was the race just hard-fought?

Did the horses near the wire show unusual degrees of fight and determination at full throttle, or just a gritty perseverance while tiring?

Did the winners run straight, or were they lugging visibly while being carried by leading jockeys?

It makes a difference; at times all the difference for in-depth class evaluation.

When Slew o' Gold, Wild Again, and Gate Dancer raced head to head through the Hollywood Park stretch of the inaugural three-million-dollar Breeders' Cup Classic, the three were widely acclaimed for providing one of the greatest finishes ever, a sheer demonstration of the highest class. It just wasn't so. The final quarter-mile was run in a slow, slow :26 3/5 seconds. Wild Again was dog tired and laboring after setting a fast pace. Slew o' Gold "hung" for one-eighth of a mile, no less. If Gate Dancer could have been kept straight by the powerful Laffit Pincay, it would have gone by the other two readily. The finish was undoubtedly exciting, but racing enthusiasts were witnessing a demonstration of grit, not class. None of the three deserved especially high marks.

The best of modern speed handicappers, the pros, have developed means of coping with the problems caused by wide variations about par. Their methods are technical and esoteric, depending for the successful application on a wide-ranging, thoughtful experience and in-depth acquaintance with the horse population at the local track.

The methods ignore par times and concentrate on the well-known times of highly consistent horses. The rating procedure relies on the concept of "projected times." Speed handicappers project today's expected final times from past performance evidence that even includes form analysis. Thus they become artistic and to some degree creative. The procedures can work provocatively in expert hands and disastrously anywhere else. Novices cannot do it. Most recreational handicappers, experience aside, cannot use the techniques effectively, and weekend players are left behind.

And in the end the matter of the intangibles remains unsettled. Intangibles separate the closest calls of class appraisal, notably when times have been superior and distances longer. Speed figures that are necesary are not sufficient. In that sense modern speed handicapping provides only a partial solution to many problems of class evaluation.

As contemporary speed handicapping became increasingly practiced, other models of handicapping that emphasized speed began to emerge. A few deserve considerable attention.

Speed points, as promoted by Bill Quirin, became a valid technique for predicting the early speed, and early speed horses were shown to win approximately 60 percent of the races at all tracks. The method relies solely on the 1st call positions and beaten lengths for three ratable races. It works wonderfully, the writer can attest.

A controversial method was labeled "ability times" by its developer William L. Scott. The method was promoted as yielding an index of speed and class in combination. The ratings rely on the final quarter-miles of sprints and the second-call intervals of middle distance routes. Raw times are modified by a carefully calibrated formula for beaten lengths and adjusted in turn by considerations of early speed and current form. Ability times next are converted into figures, as with speed charts.

Ability times as method was launched within a grand scheme for systematizing the whole of the handicapping process by steps demonstrably effective in generating profits. The method applied only to the public's first three betting choices.

The efficacy of ability times outside of its original framework remains an open debate. Many practitioners have reported consistent profits on "double advantage" horses, or selections whose top two ability times each are higher than either rating of any other contender. Probability studies confirm the experiences; the impact value of double-advantage horses approaches 2.50.

Pace as Class

Impoverished by traditional methods of speed handicapping, financially as much as intellectually, several authors of the fifties and sixties switched to pace as the quantitative approach to beating the races. Pace honored the relations among fractional times and final times. Its proponents sometimes emphasized instead the rates of speed horses could demonstrate for a specific race segment or for a combination of segments.

The varieties of pace handicapping roamed the waterfront. The early Ray Taulbot promoted pace to the half mile in sprints, to the three-quarters in routes, as the critical segments. A contemporary named Hugh Matheson argued differently, that the third quarter of sprints, the third and fourth quarters of routes, were most important. Huey Mahl gathered a huge following when he promoted a fascinating hybrid approach whereby the first quarter was combined with the final quarter.

None of the methods were accompanied by persuasive evidence of their effectiveness.

This shortcoming became painfully clear to thousands of pace analysts in 1981 when John Meyer, of the *National Railbird Review,* submitted the traditional methods of obtaining pace ratings to a computerized study encompassing thousands of races.

Meyer evaluated the relative importance of eight pace segments. He asked what percentage of winners in four types of races (dirt sprints, dirt routes, dirt miles, and grass routes) also had run at the fastest rate of speed during each of the race segments under investigation. In other words, which race segments produce the most winners?

The findings proved a body blow to all concerned. None of the favored race segments were correlated with sufficient numbers of winners to matter. Rate of speed sustained throughout an entire race outperformed the several race segments without exception. High speed from start to finish was correlated with 41 percent of the winners.

Speed to the first call was associated with more winners than any other segment or combination of segments.

Handicappers who had been concentrating their pace calculations on the final segments of races were working with only 5 percent of the winners in sprints, 10 percent in routes.

Mahl's hybrid approach performed just slightly better, associated with 19 percent of the winners.

Start to second call in sprints was the fastest segment for 22 percent of the winners of sprints but a much more substantial 43 percent of routes, an intriguing surprise.

In sum, the Meyer study indicated the relative importance of examining races in their entirety and could be interpreted to mean that pace analysis beats pace ratings. Another plausible interpretation of the data, one I prefer, is that pace ratings should complement but not displace pace analysis.

The first author to put pace in that kind of perspective was Tom Ainslie, who in promoting comprehensive handicapping used the factor to separate contenders otherwise closely matched on form, distance, and class.

Ainslie proposed a simple arithmetical procedure which abided by the classical definition of pace as the interrelationships among fractional times and final times, but the technique suffered the same flaws inherent in unmodified speed handicapping. The raw times utilized were not sufficiently accurate estimates of true speed to distinguish otherwise closely matched horses.

The failing might be corrected by placing additional stress on the interpretation, demanding large numerical differences in the ratings, but the adaptation correspondingly reduces the utility of the method. The horses to be rated, after all, had already been judged close on the other fundamentals. Unrefined pace methods permitted too many contenders to go postward still undistinguished on pace and class. More sensitive models of pace handicapping were needed still.

Following a lengthy hiatus, as speed methods dominated, pace as a fundamental factor in handicapping has enjoyed a renaissance in recent years. The factor promises to perform as not before. The new methods avoid the thorny problems of their predecessors. Not surprisingly, the microcomputer has played a vital role in the reawakening. Modern models of pace handicapping are mathematically complex. Several rely on velocity ratings, a measure of feet per second, as opposed to the conventional fractional times and fifths of seconds.

Velocity ratings dispel the equation whereby one length equals one-fifth of a second, overriding gross errors inherent in that kind of computation. A length, instead, equals nine, ten, or eleven feet. When distance is divided by time, the measure yields a much finer estimate of true speed.

By a widening margin, the most powerful model of pace handicapping today is the Sartin Methodology, which relies on velocity ratings, examines multiple race intervals, relates pace ratings to the energy demands of individual racetracks, can adjust basic ratings in multiple ways, ranks contenders on four or five measures of pace, and remains analytical and judgmental in its final decision making.

The methodology is centered on the proposition that race-

horses accelerate and decelerate individually but within predictable pace patterns, depending on the energy requirements
and biases of racetracks. The psychologist Sartin has worked
with compulsive gamblers and has been evolving his method
for years, initially in consequence of his dictum that the gamblers could only wager on horse races—because knowledge
and skill could actually result in winning the game, a percep-
tion he might usefully transmit as well in reality-therapy
groups for racetrack executives—and on races only on the provision the groups could elaborate a method of playing the races
that worked.

Two of Sartin's refinements make important bows to class.
First, ratings are restricted to horses that are suited to the eligibility conditions of races; are not outclassed. Two, an average
earnings adjustment credits horses that have been performing
well in better races. The latter is optional, as Sartin appreciates
it can mislead users as well.

A user of my acquaintance takes an additional step when analyzing severe dropdowns in claiming races. He compares the
best performance of the highest priced claiming race in the recent record with the customary pace ratings of other contenders. If the dropdown's rating in the superior race is not best, my
friend is inclined to wager against the larger class drops, and
absolutely so at low odds.

In the summer of 1985, Sartin, who maintains a bird's-eye
view of his following, listed approximately 800 steady clients,
and he said exactly 619 of them had demonstrated profits—become winners—at least for a time.

The Sartin Methodology is complicated and requires high-
tech support but can be implemented more readily than
understood, as is customarily true of high-tech models of complicated matters, such as handicapping. Sartin's method, as far
as the author knows, supplies its devotees with the most accurate, most powerful pace ratings on the American racing scene.
The ratings are not interchangeable with class ratings; but if
the pace lines selected for analysis represent the competitive
levels of horses well, they accomplish the desirable distinctions.

A natural extension of the modern advances in speed handicapping is to pace handicapping. Bill Quirin has led the way. Quirin has shown handicappers how to construct pace pars, by apportioning the fifths of seconds of final times to tenths of seconds in calculating half-mile pars in sprints and six-furlongs pars in routes.

In researching his extended methods, Quirin has identified nine typical "race shapes" he calls configurations of pace. They are labeled fast-average-slow at both the fractional par and final par, such that a fast-fast pace is two lengths (or more) faster than par at both intervals. A fast-average pace is two lengths fast to the half but typical in the end, and slow-slow means two lengths slower than normal at both intervals.

Quirin implores handicappers accustomed to speed figures not to sum the two ratings but to eyeball them analytically, in terms of the running styles that should benefit from the respective race shapes. A fast-slow shape, for instance, favors closers and a slow-fast shape favors frontrunners. Quirin reinforces the argument that pace analysis supersedes pace ratings.

As an aside, numerous personal applications of race shapes as method at Santa Anita indicate unmistakably that in claiming races the fast-fast shapes can be counted upon to beat the others repeatedly.

Pace as a reflection of class has begun to erase its sullied past, as did speed handicapping, and today enjoys sizeable advantages in a game evermore tilted toward its speedier horses. The new methods work, and in expert hands become powerful enough to throw consistent seasonal profits.

Earnings as Class

The traditional referents of class have suffered a modern fate practically opposite the improvements attaching to contemporary speed and pace handicapping.

Once upon a time just a decade ago, gross earnings remained strongly associated with probable winners. The top earners in a field won 150 percent their rightful share of the races and were three times more likely to win than were low earners. Five years later these probability values not only had tailed off but were much less pregnant with meaning. The public normally overbets the high earners. As a group they accumulate losses upward of 30 percent.

By the 1980s, moreover. the top half of a field's moneymakers were winning only slightly more races than the bottom half, while throwing losses of 15 percent. By 1985, a single win by a well-placed two- or three-year-old could propel it atop the earnings standings for half a season, and a couple of those wins could stamp a horse as one of the leading moneymakers of all time.

Average earnings has traditionally outperformed gross earnings as a predictor of race outcomes, although not significantly. Even here, however, the top-ranked horses have lost approximately 8 percent on investment. When horses ranked first in average earnings also showed a "good" race last out, the probability they will win improves to 225 percent. Yet they lose money still; 5 percent. The public likes to bet on high-earning horses.

Of these indices times have changed for the worse, at least so far as class handicapping is involved. The next round of probability studies will reveal the diminishing potency of earning power as an index of class. Purse inflation has subverted all claims to legitimacy where comparative earnings are evaluated. Instability among purse structures is running rampant throughout the racing industry. At any successful major meeting the purses near the end of the meeting will be significantly higher for the same races than at the start. Stakes races continue to multiply abundantly, their larger purse strings dangled like magnets to attract the better stables.

Garden State, in New Jersey, launched its third-generation racetrack with one of the most lucrative stakes programs in the country. Not a single added-money event dipped below $50,000. The Jersey Derby offered the nation's three-year-olds their first million-dollar purse, not to mention the two-million-dollar bonus that would eventually threaten the complexion of the sport's Triple Crown. Other stakes' purses were boosted. The money worked its wonders with horsemen. Notwithstanding attendance and handle figures below expectation, Garden State is back on the thoroughbred map, a major meeting.

The first racetrack in Minnesota, Canterbury Downs, in Shakopee, near Minneapolis, during its baptismal seduced the nation's leading sprinters with the $100,000-added Chaucer Cup,
older horses with the $150,000-guaranteed Canterbury Cup,
and those battling three-year-olds with the $150,000-guaran-
teed Canterbury Derby. The three races should become graded
stakes within the minimum two years, thanks to the money.
Six other stakes offered minor Midwest stables $50,000-added.
The overall purse structure devised by director of racing Louis
Eilken was appealing enough to lure established stables, trainers, and jockeys from all points in the Midwest and South, as
well as a few key stables and jockeys from as far away as California.

Canterbury's second season (1986) saw leading horsemen
D. Wayne Lukas and Jack Van Berg send major divisions to
Shakopee. The $150,000-guaranteed Canterbury Derby became
the $300,000-guaranteed St. Paul Derby, and Preakness winner
Snow Chief was almost flown there to get the money.

In addition, almost all racetracks now cater to statewide
breeding industries struggling to enhance the commercial
value of the local stud. The tracks card more races and stakes
limited to state-breds. They have to. They need the horses. The
money is huge. State-bred overnite purses normally exceed the
value of comparable open races. State-bred horses that never
win an open race can earn important money in the modern
sport.

Established racetracks respond to new competition they face
incessantly from inside the sport and outside gaming interests
as well by raising the ante as best they can. Purses will continue to climb. Stakes will continue to multiply. Cheaper
horses will be earning bigger money still in a dangerous cycle
of inter-track competition.

So average earnings of ordinary horses have not just crept
upward in the manner of a linear progression. They have
spurted upward, shot through the ceiling, gone haywire.

Furthermore, the time-honored stability of racetrack purse
structures is now out of fashion. Two-year-olds will soon be
million-dollar babies. At this writing the second-leading money
winner of all time is a three-year-old having four months left

in the season. Older horses are getting more, too, but the real windfalls for four-year-olds and up depends either on bonus money or a Breeders' Cup score. Comparatively, older horses are fast becoming the poorer brothers and sisters.

With purse structures out of balance and the competition among racetracks intensifying, the correlation between average earnings and the class of the field inexorably approaches zero. In certain fields of younger horses it's plausible that gross earnings could represent an inverse relationship to real abilities.

In a valiant but beleaguered attempt to develop a more sensitive measure of earnings as a predictor of class, several authors of the early eighties recommended the earnings box be submitted to an apparently clever brand of arithmetic, in contrast to summing or averaging. The idea was to identify the *average purse value* for which horses have been able to compete successfully.

The desired value is obtained by multiplying the number of times horses have finished first, second, third, and fourth by the percentage of the purse each placing earns. Purse structures vary among states, but for illustration here first finishes can be multiplied by .60, second finishes by .22, third finishes by .12, and fourth finishes by .06. The products are summed. The sum is divided into gross earnings. The quotient represents the purse value a horse has "competed successfully for," presumably a more sensitive index of relative class.

Unfortunately, the presumption does not hold. First, probability studies have shown *a priori* that average purse value is the weakest of the basic approaches to class appraisal utilizing earning power. Gross earnings and average earnings do better as predictors. Moreover, mathematician Bill Quirin has revealed just how misleading a reliance on average purse values can be.

Consider the table below:

$$\$15,000/.60 = \$25,000$$
$$5,500/.22 = 25,000$$
$$3,000/.12 = 25,000$$
$$1,500/.06 = 25,000$$

The dollar amounts indicate how a $25,000 purse of New York is divided, with 60 percent belonging to the winner.

As can be seen, the rating formula allows a first starter to be rated equally whether it finishes first or fourth. Assuming this is the first race completed by the winner, it will be rated 25 (1/1000th of a $25,000 purse), as .60 × 1 = .60 and $15,000 in earnings divided by .60 equals a $25,000 purse value, the amount the winner has competed successfully for.

If the same horse had finished fourth, however, it would still be rated 25, as the fourth share of $1500 divided by .06 equals the same $25,000 purse value.

As Quirin points out, the method's fatal flaw is the inability to discriminate among "successful" horses. To drive the point across, Quirin presents the following hypothetical tables of four horses that have started ten times each, along with their number of wins, seconds, thirds, fourths, and total earnings:

Horse A	10-10-0-0-0	$150,000
Horse B	10-0-10-0-0	55,000
Horse C	10-0-0-10-0	30,000
Horse D	10-0-0-0-10	15,000

Again using the New York purse structure, each horse would be rated 25, for "competing successfully" for purses of $25,000.

To reach for the ludicrous extension of a flawed procedure, Quirin next presents Horse E: 10-1-0-0-0 and $15,000. A horse that wins one race in ten and finishes out of the money otherwise is rated—you guessed it—25, a purse value of $25,000, the same as Horse A, which won ten of ten.

So the average purse value formulas will confuse the issue far more frequently than they clarify it. The method can be extremely unfair in one way or another to younger, lightly raced horses and unfairly generous to older horses that finish close consistently without winning, the latter type a despicable genre to class handicappers.

As matters stand now, earnings power has lost significant credibility as a reliable index of relative class. There is a lesson here. Class handicappers best rely on assessing real abilities and not on the traditional referents of those abilities. Referents such as gross earnings, average earnings, and average purse values will always be susceptible to winds of change. The more detached from actual abilities the referents become, the greater the havoc wreaked by the changes.

To less extent, the same erosion of credibility has afflicted our next topic, claiming prices.

Claiming Price Comparisons as Class

Until the 1980s, class handicappers understood correctly that claiming horses dropping in selling price had a far better chance to win than horses rising in price. The 1974 probability studies of Fred Davis revealed that a selling-price slash of 30 percent or more had an impact value (I.V.) of 3.78—won almost four times the fair share of their starts—the strongest probability statistic in classical handicapping.

By 1979 and Quirin's probability studies, that I.V. had dropped to 1.27, but if the dropdown followed a "good" race, it rose again to 2.07. Class drops among claiming horses still count, all right, but the claiming game has changed radically.

Quirin's data indicated that claiming horses moving up and down a level or remaining at the same level were able to win equally well. Actually, the class step-ups had a slight advantage. Even horses moving up by two claiming levels won 85 percent of the fair share of their races, not a pessimistic statistic.

It's clear that claiming horses of today move up and down in class successfully as never before. Several factors explain the phenomenon.

Form cycles vary more capriciously across the longer, harsher seasons, a huge factor.

As a consequence of more racing dates too, cheaper horses experience more soundness and fitness problems. Cheaper horses are also more abundant, with thousands more of them racing than just a decade ago.

Shipping has increased terrifically, even among claiming horses of the same or nearby circuits.

Most important of all, three-year-olds now populate the

claiming divisions at major tracks as never before, and these developing horses are still forming actual abilities, distance preferences, and pace preferences. Class levels are not yet understood, and stable maneuverings become continuous. In the fall the same jostling of platers and prices dominates the juvenile divisions.

Probability data suggest a practical remedy for making tenable the claiming price comparisons. Where comparisons must preside, as I have suggested elsewhere, handicappers best think in terms of claiming price brackets, or ranges of selling prices within which horses can be expected to perform well. Class maneuvers within brackets can be accepted as constituting no significant change in relative class, but moves outside of familiar brackets represent a real change in the order of competition.

By this convention, at most tracks the claiming class changes, up or down, of one level, perhaps two, would be accepted as staying within accustomed ranges of competitiveness, but changes of one, two, or three levels, when perceived as ranging outside of hospitable brackets, would not. This practice remains highly compatible with the latest evidence.

Yet a fundamental problem of claiming class appraisal remains firmly intact. The tendency of claiming races to deal exclusively in speed duels makes price comparisons insensitive to the distinctions of most interest. Far more often than not, the intangibles of class do not come vividly into play in the cheaper races. The exceptions tend to be so conspicuous in the determination and willingness on display the races prove the rule.

So handicappers who want to prepare for class maneuvers in the modern claiming game are best advised first, to identify the brackets characteristic of the local scene and second, to calculate speed figures or pace ratings. The quantitative methods often will identify the class-within-a-class for the various claiming brackets. When they do not, the class ratings promoted here complete the task. A multifaceted approach is probably best.

Comparison Handicapping and Class

Whenever a highly touted developing racehorse clobbers its opposition by many lengths in rapid time, the same horsemen who deride the importance of time will question the talents of the horses left behind. "He wasn't beating much," is the throw-away remark, implying the result may be radically different when the upstart meets its own kind. The Runyonesque translation of the horseman's lament reverberates throughout the grandstand: "He didn't beat nothin'!"

Both camps are proponents of comparison handicapping, the timeless notion that a thoroughbred's true class can be determined only by the caliber of horses it has beaten.

Is the point well taken?

It's a double-edged sword. Yes, provided the past performance tables contain stable estimates of relative abilities, speed quotients, distance and pace preferences, and form cycles. This is normally true only of older horses, four-year-olds and older. The wealth of information renders the crucial comparisons facile. If a five-year-old wallops a field that has not amounted to much, the result next out may surely be a reversal.

The other side of the response must be tentative and inconclusive. Where the past performances do not yet provide reliable indices of real abilities, manner of victory can be more persuasive than victory itself. It can also be convincingly deceptive. This is characteristic of nonclaiming three-year-olds, the most complicating of thoroughbreds, and of two-year-olds at the route.

The classic situation is the three-year-old that has won wire-to-wire in sizzling time. What will happen next? It's often hard to predict. Horsemen who insist the creature had nothing in its dust, although stating the obvious, may prove prophetic. They might also be missing clues as obvious as the margin of victory, such as a fast-fast shape at every call plus visible reserves of speed and energy at the finish.

Horsemen that debunked the exploit and adopted a wait-and-see attitude following Spend A Buck's powerful win, easily consummated, in the 1985 Kentucky Derby did not know what they were talking about. Regardless of long experience, they do not qualify as expert comparison handicappers. The colt that ran wire-to-wire that May was absolutely the outstanding member of its class, as anyone informed would have seen.

So comparison handicapping has traditionally worked well enough when evaluating older horses and not so well with younger developing horses. The generality itself is precarious. Was that impressive six-length victory a product of the winner's unmistakable brilliance or were its chief antagonists just off their game?

A class handicapping technique that sometimes solves this riddle *ex post facto* was promoted years ago by professional handicapper and author Steve Davidowitz. It is the Key Race Method.

As Davidowitz explained, the method is designed to reveal class within a class. Its peculiar feature achieves the goal by discounting a comparison between horses and substituting a comparison between races. The key race occurs at any class level where a race has proved to be intensely competitive, as indicated by the next-out victories of multiple horses in the field. The graduates of key races can be expected to win and win again, and they do.

For an extraordinary illustration of the Key Race Method, examine the result chart on page 55. The key race, a graded stakes, occurred during Santa Anita 1985. The circled horses graduated from the race to win the next time.

Class handicappers who had isolated Santa Anita's 1985 Sierra Madre Handicap (Grade 3) as a key race later spotted successive opportunities to bet on seven of the race's graduates. Several won repeatedly. The winner, Forzando II, eventually won Belmont Park's Grade 1 Metropolitan Mile Handicap as the longshot in the cast.

To implement the Key Race Method, handicappers need only a set of result charts. Circle the names of the winners of the most recent 60–70 races in the charts of their previous races. As indicated by the circles, look for races boasting multiple winners next out. A pattern preferred by many handicappers finds

EIGHTH RACE
Santa Anita
FEBRUARY 11, 1985

ABOUT 6 ½ FURLONGS:(Turf). (1.11⅗) 22nd Running of THE SIERRA MADRE HANDICAP (Grade III). $60,000 added. 4-year-olds and upward. By subscription of $50 each to accompany the nomination, $100 to pass the entry box and $600 to start, with $60,000 added, of which $12,000 to second, $9,000 to third, $4,500 to fourth and $1,500 to fifth. Weights, Wednesday, February 6. Starters to be named through the entry box by the closing time of entries. A trophy will be presented to the owner of the winner. Closed Wednesday, January 30, 1985 with 25 nominations. Value of race $71,250; value to winner $44,250; second $12,000; third $9,000; fourth $4,500; fifth $1,500. Mutuel pool $691,138.

Last Raced	Horse	Eqt.	A.	Wt	PP	St	¼	½	Str	Fin	Jockey	Odds $1
27Jan85 ^{5}SA^4	Forzando II		4	117	1	13	11^{hd}	12^{5}	$6^{1\frac{1}{2}}$	$1^{\frac{1}{2}}$	Toro F	11.80
3Feb85 ^{5}SA^1	Lucky Buccaneer		4	117	2	5	4^{hd}	3^{hd}	$2^{2\frac{1}{2}}$	$2^{1\frac{1}{2}}$	Pedroza M A	9.30
23Jan85 ^{5}SA^1	Champagne Bid	b	6	121	10	3	$2^{2\frac{1}{2}}$	1^{hd}	$1^{\frac{1}{2}}$	$3^{\frac{1}{2}}$	Sibille R	2.70
27Jan85 ^{5}SA^2	Ayman		5	117	5	10	9^{hd}	$10^{1\frac{1}{2}}$	$7^{\frac{1}{2}}$	4^{hd}	Pincay L Jr	5.90
27Jan85 ^{5}SA^5	Patrick McFig		6	115	4	6	5^{hd}	$5^{\frac{1}{2}}$	3^{hd}	5^{nk}	McHargue D G	46.90
26Jan85 ^{5}SA^6	Wise Strategy	b	5	114	3	14	13^{6}	13^{4}	13^{1}	$6^{\frac{1}{2}}$	McGurn C	f-28.90
19Jan85 ^{8}BM^7	Algardi	b	6	111	13	12	14	14	14	7^{hd}	Dominguez R L	f-28.90
27Jan85 ^{5}SA^3	Rocky Marriage	b	5	116	8	2	10^{2}	8^{hd}	$9^{1\frac{1}{2}}$	8^{hd}	Delahoussaye E	17.00
25Jan85 ^{8}SA^1	Retsina Run	b	5	116	9	11	12^{6}	11^{1}	10^{hd}	9^{nk}	Meza R Q	16.50
30Dec84 ^{8}SA^4	Laughing Boy	b	7	113	11	8	8^{hd}	$9^{\frac{1}{2}}$	12^{2}	10^{nk}	McCarron C J	28.90
26Jan85 ^{8}SA^{11}	Fifty Six Ina Row		4	115	6	7	$7^{2\frac{1}{2}}$	7^{2}	8^{hd}	11no	Stevens G L	9.60
27Jan85 ^{5}SA^1	Shananie		6	121	7	4	3^{hd}	4^{2}	$5^{\frac{1}{2}}$	$12^{1\frac{1}{2}}$	Hawley S	3.50
23Jan85 ^{5}SA^4	Rivets Factor	b	7	114	12	9	$6^{\frac{1}{2}}$	$6^{2\frac{1}{2}}$	11^{hd}	13^{2}	Olivares F	f-28.90
21Jan85 ^{7}SA^3	Maxim Gorky		7	116	14	1	1^{hd}	2^{2}	4^{hd}	14	Shoemaker W	11.30

f—Mutuel field.

OFF AT 4:26 Start good. Won driving. Time, :20⅘, :43, 1:07, 1:14⅘ Course firm.

$2 Mutuel Prices:			
1–FORZANDO II	25.60	14.20	7.20
2–LUCKY BUCCANEER		10.20	7.20
9–CHAMPAGNE BID			3.80

B. c, by Formidable—Princely Maid, by King's Troop. Trainer Sullivan John. Bred by Red House Stud (Eng).

FORZANDO II saved ground while lacking early speed, found room to rally on the rail in the stretch, angled outside the leaders in the final sixteenth and was up in the closing strides. LUCKY BUCCANEER, in contention from the outset, also responded outside the leaders in the stretch drive, got the lead in the final sixteenth but could not outfinish the winner. CHAMPAGNE BID forced the early pace inside MAXIM GORKY, got the advantage on the second turn but hung near the end. AYMAN offered a strong but belated rally near the rail through the stretch. PATRICK MCFIG, in contention and saving ground for a half, lacked the needed rally. WISE STRATEGY and ALGARDI rallied wide but finished strongly. FIFTY SIX INA ROW, in contention for a half, lacked the needed closing response. SHANANIE, in good position for a half, tired in the stretch, as did RIVETS FACTOR. MAXIM GORKY set or forced the pace outside CHAMPAGNE BID to the stretch and stopped.

Owners— 1, Paniolo Rch-Cale-Tuerk et al; 2, Narvaez G & Coraleen; 3, Saddle Hill Farm; 4, Happy Valley Farm & Peskoff; 5, Newman B; 6, MeadowView Fm & Ventura St; 7, Mandysland Farm; 8, Port & Ramos; 9, Oldknow & Phipps; 10, Elmendorf Farm Inc; 11, Valpredo J; 12, Fuller P; 13, Millstream Stable, 14, Wong S G.

Trainers— 1, Sullivan John; 2, Stute Melvin F; 3, Winick Randy; 4, Barrera Lazaro S; 5, French Neil; 6, Whittingham Michael; 7, Drysdale Neil; 8, Frankel Robert; 9, Rettele Loren; 10, Jones Gary; 11, Guiney Irv Jr; 12, Russell John W; 13, Landers Dale; 14, Palma Hector O.

Overweight: Ayman 1 pound; Patrick McFig 1; Wise Strategy 4; Rocky Marriage 1; Rivets Factor 2.

Scratched—Delta Trace (30Dec84 ^{8}BM^5); Doria's Delight (3Feb85 ^{5}SA^4).

a next-out victory by a race's winner and its fourth- or fifth-place finisher. They await eagerly the horses that finished in between, notably if the key race were hotly contested or the time lickety-split. The method works especially well with maiden races and turf races, where the available information about relative class tends to be spottier and the resulting comparisons trickier.

Comparison handicapping involving younger nonclaiming horses is typically a far more difficult art. No historical methods of class handicapping that assess real abilities exist, other than observation skills that might perceive the fine com-

petitive differences between leading horses and the ordinary
hundreds.

An intention of this book is to supply handicappers with a
rating method that can compare nonclaiming three-year-olds
on the severally joined attributes of class. Below is an instructive illustration of the possibilities the approach I have in mind
entails. Examine the result chart carefully. Par for the class-
distance category is 1:17 1/5 seconds. The daily variant March
16 at Santa Anita was Fast 1. What kinds of comparisons can
you detect?

FOURTH RACE

Santa Anita

MARCH 16, 1985

6 ½ FURLONGS. (1.14) ALLOWANCE. Purse $23,000. Colts and geldings. 3-year-olds which
are non-winners of $2,500 other than maiden or claiming. Weight, 120 lbs. Non-winners other
than claiming since December 25 allowed 3 lbs.; of such a race since November 6, 6 lbs.

Value of race $23,000; value to winner $12,650; second $4,600; third $3,450; fourth $1,725; fifth $575. Mutuel pool $344,809.
Exacta Pool $477,867.

Last Raced	Horse	Eqt.A.Wt PP St	¼	½	Str	Fin	Jockey	Odds $1
23Feb85 ⁶SA¹	Phone Trick	b 3 120 2 4	1²	1²	1½	12½	Pincay L Jr	.70
2Mar85 ⁶SA¹	Pancho Villa	b 3 120 5 5	44½	2ʰᵈ	2³	22½	McHargue D G	8.40
3Mar85 ⁶SA⁶	Palestine Sun	b 3 114 4 2	6	52½	4⁶	3³	Hawley S	19.60
27Feb85 ⁸SA²	Colt Forty Four	3 120 3 3	2½	3²	3¹	46½	Delahoussaye E	2.30
24Feb85¹⁰TuP⁴	Mr. Thomas	3 120 1 6	3¹½	41½	5ʰᵈ	52½	McCarron C J	8.80
1Nov84 ⁶BM³	On The Shorts	3 114 6 1	5ʰᵈ	6	6	6	Stevens G L	13.50

OFF AT 2:46. Start good. Won driving. Time, :21, :43⅗, 1:09, 1:15⅗ Track fast.

$2 Mutuel Prices:

2-PHONE TRICK	3.40	2.80	2.80
5-PANCHO VILLA		5.40	4.00
4-PALESTINE SUN			5.60

$5 EXACTA 2-5 PAID $49.50.

B. c, by Clever Trick—Over the Phone, by Finnegan. Trainer Mandella Richard. Bred by Lanier B (Ky).

PHONE TRICK was rated through the quick early fractions, turned back a bid from PANCHO VILLA leaving
the furlong pole and was drawing off at the finish. PANCHO VILLA, outrun early, lodged a strong bid to contention
on the far turn, got closest to the winner nearing the furlong pole and flattened out. PALESTINE SUN raced evenly.
COLT FORTY FOUR prompted the early pace and steadily tired after a half. MR. THOMAS, a bit slow to gain at the
start, was finished early. ON THE SHORTS was outrun.

Owners— 1, DeAngelis-Mndlla-Wynne; 2, French Jr & Lukas; 3, Jones K; 4, Van Berg J C; 5, House M; 6,
H & H Stable.

Trainers— 1, Mandella Richard; 2, Lukas D Wayne; 3, Rettele Loren; 4, Van Berg Jack C; 5, Landers Dale;
6, Ward Gary.

The conditions of eligibility admit only nonwinners of a single allowance race, unless the first share were so small the
winner must have shipped to Santa Anita from minor feeder
tracks, or perhaps South America.

In March the conditions are elementary for better threes at
Santa Anita, the first step outside of the maiden ranks. Yet this
sprint qualifies as the most competitive among classier three-
year-olds during the entire Santa Anita season. The pace was

remarkable, the final time the fastest of the season under the conditions. The adjusted final time was six lengths faster than par and better than par for any nonclaiming conditions below stakes. It was just one tick slower than the stakes par for three-year-olds. Moreover, the challenge of Pancho Villa between the pre-stretch and stretch calls was superb and sustained.

The D. Wayne Lukas colt came charging at the frontrunner, which already had burned out a :21 flat first quarter. The two knocked heads until the sixteenth pole, at which point the amazing Phone Trick pulled away again. On every attribute of class, the first two finishers earned the highest ratings possible. They soared immediately to the head of the sophomore sprint division.

The class ratings became unusually advantageous a week later, when trainer Lukas shipped Pancho Villa to New York and aggressively entered the colt in the seven-furlong Grade 2 Bay Shore stakes at Aqueduct. It was a smart, timely maneuver by Lukas. Few Grade 2 sprints appear on the national agenda.

The New York handicappers saw a speedy colt that had just lost an allowance affair for nonwinners other than maiden or claiming and was now moving into graded stakes competition. By conventional handicapping, they ignored the shipper. Wrong. By the rating method promoted here Pancho Villa had earned a performance index twice as great as normal and a class ranking near the top of the division. By its adjusted time and competitive quality Pancho Villa had earned the highest class rating available under the conditions, running second to the most ferocious three-year-old sprinter on the grounds in the fastest six-and-one-half furlongs of the season.

A comparison of similar class ratings with other horses in the Bay Shore would have revealed whether any had shown as much promise at that preliminary stage. It would reveal as well how impressively the others had progressed to the Grade 2 level.

The rating method to be described here promotes exactly those types of comparisons of demonstrated abilities. It fills a huge void in handicapping discourse that will be exploited expertly by modern class handicappers. Pancho Villa broke slowly in New York's Bay Shore but won the race smashingly. The final time and manner of victory literally startled New Yorkers, and some went so far as to propel the Lukas colt into the national picture as a Triple Crown prospect. The mutuel was $30.80

The New Yorkers abandoned the center on all points. The Bay Shore outcome was entirely predictable by class handicapping, but the same kind of handicapping would not dare intimate the sensational-sprinting Pancho Villa had suddenly propelled itself into a favorite's role for the three-year-old classics.

As the Pancho Villa example confirms, the conventional methods used to clarify class and obtain class ratings are no longer tenable. They have been revealed variously to be unsubstantial, incomplete, and inconsequential. They have served mainly to lead "class" handicappers closer to the poorhouse and to insure that class handicapping would eventually take a backseat to other systematic methods perceived by practitioners as more helpful and rewarding.

Today class handicapping performs as second banana to the modern varieties of speed handicapping, pace handicapping, trip handicapping, and the hybrid methods emphasizing those factors. But class handicapping is inherently more vital and valuable than that and begs to become fashionable once again.

The remainder of this book is concerned with solving that problem by providing class handicappers a remedy long overdue.

4

Strategy for a Remedy

The preceding discussion anticipates a full-bodied strategy for obtaining contemporary class ratings which avoid the pratfalls of their predecessors. The strategy must satisfy six criteria:

1. Assesses real abilities.
2. Encompasses the several attributes of class in combination: speed-endurance-competitiveness.
3. Integrates the quantitative and qualitative aspects of performance.
4. Reflects ability in relation to specific levels of opposition.
5. Distinguishes horses within a specific category of competition; that is, assesses class within a class.
6. Is adjustable to new levels of opposition.

A practical imperative is that the rating method be easy to understand, apply, and record by recreational handicappers.

Numerous attempts to succeed in these directions have resulted in what might be conveniently coined the 100-Point Blueboy method. The ultimate rating will be 100 points, a standard to which other horses can be readily referenced. Bluebloods, of course, are the sons and daughters of the sport's most successful sires, members of its aristocratic families. The best performers on the track become potential bluebloods themselves. *Blueboy* is a tortured extension of the term, applicable to better racehorses.

Here are the method's broadstrokes:

1. Invokes the well-ordered conditions of eligibility to define the progressively difficult nature of the competition. Assigns class-speed points between levels and within levels as well.
2. Computes numerical class ratings that reflect performance at each of the respective levels of the competition.
3. Uses well-known class-distance pars *plus* the typical variations above and below par as the objective standards of speed.
4. Uses the operationally defined points of a Competitive Quality Scale to rate the quality of performance demonstrated at any particular level of the competition.
5. Produces basic ratings by the multiplication of the speed-class points and competitiveness ratings.
6. Controls for degrees of endurance by rating sprints and routes separately; that is, ratings are not interchangeable with distance changes.
7. Uses a simple arithmetical procedure to adjust basic ratings to new levels of competition (conditions of eligibility).
8. Uses a purse value index to adjust basic ratings for racetrack class.

Handicappers should pause here to associate the broad outlines of the method with the criteria of the general strategy.

Implementation Keys

Several keys to the efficacy of the method should be stressed.

First, the method assigns a scale of class-speed points to each of the respective conditions of eligibility. The differences among the scale points must reflect simultaneously

a. the increasingly strenuous speed demands at each succeeding level of opposition.

b. the range of performance (final times) that has been typical within each level.

The gradations of difficulty between and within the various levels become the essential referents for obtaining finer estimates of relative class. Fortunately, the speed quotients between and within levels have been well known for some time. The method builds on that documentation.

Second, the points of the Competitive Quality Scale must be defined concretely using guidelines that are both internally logical and consistent and serve well to reduce the subjective character of the rating procedure. To the extent that various well-schooled users obtain different class ratings, or the individual user's ratings of the same kinds of performances differ at different points in time, the desired objectivity of the method will be eroded. Inter-rater reliability must be satisfactorily high.

The method must be sensitive and powerful enough to distinguish real class differences both between and within classes. Such differences can be small or great. Ratings methods customarily fall down on the distinctions, generating small numerical differences in all cases. By this book's method, where real differences in performance are seen to be greater, the small numerical differences normally associated with speed-pace rating methods will be replaced by greater differences.

On the other hand, any obvious distinctions suggested by ratings must reflect real distinctions or the game has been lost again.

The Blueboy method makes concessions to errors of the latter type in order to detect real differences in class that are larger. The matter is especially critical where younger developing horses will be evaluated. These horses too often earn comparable speed-pace ratings where real differences in ability exist. The book's method is designed to identify precisely those greater differences.

Finally, the means employed to reflect the relative nature of thoroughbred class must modify ratings previously earned when a new order of competition is faced. This too takes on far greater impact with rating young horses, notably nonclaiming horses, which are merely following a path toward true levels of competition. Where basic ratings have been artificially inflated or reduced, as when derived from performances unrelated to today's typical class demands, users will be sorrowfully misled. The book's final chapter tells how to adjust basic ratings when comparing younger developing horses that are competing under conditions not readily comparable, as from the maiden win to a restricted stakes.

The several keys to effective implementation suggest the practical reason the history of class methodology has been so jumbled and misguided. The task is extremely complicated and any resulting method of rating class comes modestly to the marketplace, knowing it will be regarded as widely for its imperfections as it might be for its strengths.

Strengths and Weaknesses

Handicappers might be persuaded that the logic underlying the book's rating method reveals its three main strengths:

1. It assesses the several attributes of class in combination and depends upon handicappers' rating real abilities that have been demonstrated in competition.
2. It integrates satisfactorily the quantitative or objective aspect of class—speed—with the qualitative or subjective aspects of class—willingness, determination, courage.
3. Within specific categories of class, it credits above-average and below-average performance in ways that can magnify real distinctions in class at the same level of opposition.

At the same time, the method discounts a crucial attribute of class, its dynamic elements. Class is strongly influenced not only by changes in the order of opposition, its relative aspect, but by variations in horses' fitness, soundness, and competitive seasoning. The book's method does not control for any dynamic changes in class due to changes in form. Form analysis therefore must supplement class evaluation in a nonmechanistic, analytical, judgmental way—the classical procedure, if you will. This book's ratings are neither increased nor reduced by form analysis, but high-rated horses might be variously discounted or preferred by form analysis. The classical handicapping view of demonstrated class as a function of current form is not included here, but is not intended to be lost.

This omission, as intimated earlier, is surely not the weak link nowadays as in times recently past. Class is less a function of good form today than ever. Standards of acceptable form have been roundly liberalized, and "acceptable" form has become the operative condition much of the time.

Let's assert that handicappers capable of a well-grounded analysis of modern thoroughbred form cycles will not be easily misguided in any event.

A constraint—not a weakness—of the method is that recreational handicappers who do not attend regularly will need off-site opportunities to watch the races. Charts are not enough. Fortunately, television replays following a day's program are more plentiful than ever. They may soon proliferate as racetrack marketing departments increasingly resort to cable systems and simulcasting to carry their product to the people.

Regardless, the present method retains its several advantages for interested handicappers. It supplies modern class ratings not available until now. When interpreted and used intelligently, as later chapters tell, the ratings represent a new, nicely wrapped procedure in the contemporary handicapper's bag of tricks.

The next chapter provides a close-up view of the method's numerical scales and rating procedures.

5

Class Ratings

It should surprise no one that a method rating class should consider first the brilliance horses can demonstrate at the various conditions of eligibility in major racing.

Examine Table 1. It represents the numerical basis for rating all nonclaiming thoroughbreds.

Step 1: Assigning Class-Speed Points

The table assigns points from 2 to 20 depending upon a horse's adjusted speed in relation to class-distance pars for eight levels of progressively challenging nonclaiming competition. Claiming races will be treated later in the chapter.

Speed quotients below par earn fewer points than par, and speed quotients above par earn more points. The row points at each level are intended to distinguish class within a class, hardly an unimportant matter, as demonstrated by final speed.

As horses progress through the array of eligibility conditions, they earn more points. The point differences between levels are intended to reflect the gradations of difficulty among various classes of competition. Where within-class differences are held greater than between-class differences, class categories were paired, as with the stakes hierarchy. By this mechanism past performances are correlated to typical class demands. The distribution of points by levels was modified several times during the tryout phase.

Notice the stakes races reflect a three-level hierarchy, ranging from restricted stakes to Grade 1 events. A Grade 1 winner that has run three lengths faster than par earns four points more than a winner that runs comparably as fast in an open stakes. A Grade 1 winner that runs an adjusted 1:34 2/5 mile at Local Downs, where the stakes par is 1:36, earns 20 brilliance points. An open stakes winner there clocking the same time earns 16 brilliance points, a concession to the weaker competi-

TABLE 1
Class-Speed Points for 8 Levels
of Nonclaiming Competition

Conditions of Eligibility	Variations About Par, All Distances				
	Par −5	Par −2, −4	Par ±1	Par +2, +4	Par +5
Maiden	2	4	5	6	7
Alw NW1xMC	3	5	7	8	9
Alw NW2xMC	4	6	8	9	10
Alw NW3xMC NW4xMC	5	8	9	10	12
Clf Alw	6	9	10	12	13
Stk Restricted (R) Open	7	10	12	14	16
Stk Listed (L) Grade 3	10	12	14	16	18
Stk Grade 2 Grade 1	12	14	16	18	20

Legend: Alw NW1xMC Allowance race, for nonwinners of a race other than maiden or claiming race, et al.

Clf Alw A classified allowance race

Stk A stakes race

Par −5 A race whose adjusted final time is five lengths or more slower than the class-distance par

Par ±1 A race whose adjusted final time equals par or ranges from one length slower to one length faster than par

Par +5 A race whose adjusted final time is five lengths or more faster than the class-distance par

tion. The procedure presupposes that listed and graded stakes winners normally run faster than open stakes horses, which they do.

The same adjusted mile time earned in the nonwinners allowance series would get 9 to 12 points only. Thus the spread of brilliance points across the eligibility spectrum is intended to illuminate relative class distinctions that the same or comparable final times too often can obscure. These differences enlarge as the competitiveness of races intensifies.

Notice, too, the scale points overlap considerably between closely related levels, as do final times and the performances they are intended to represent. Thus strong performances at a lower class level earn more points than average or weak performances at the next higher level. Successful rises in class not only become more predictable, but also more readily distinguished from step-ups destined to fail. Point differences reveal actual differences.

Handicappers need local class-distance par times and daily track variants to obtain the adjusted final times from which they can assign class-speed points for brilliance. Par times are now available at low cost.

Pars in hand, daily track variants can be calculated within minutes for sprints and routes from the raw times reported by *Daily Racing Form* result charts or published by newspapers. Sensible guidelines and procedures for calculating daily variants have been widely dispersed and will not be reiterated here. Newcomers are referred to excellent texts by Andrew Beyer and William L. Quirin.

Step 2: Rating the Competitive Quality of Races

A five-point Likert-type scale* is recommended to rate a race's competitive quality. Let's call it exactly that: the Competitive Quality Scale (CQ).

* A scale of ordered points having no value at absolute zero and roughly equivalent intervals between point values.

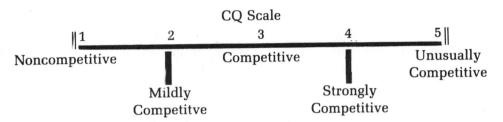

The points on the scale not only are ordered but also the intervals between points are roughly equivalent in reflecting the degrees of the attribute being assessed. Each point must be defined operationally, meaning highly specific descriptions of the kinds of races that warrant each point value. Handicappers will find those descriptions in the next chapter.

The scale indicates a typical *competitive* performance is rated 3. What is typical?

We postulate a basic definition and two variations of it. A *competitive* race consists of a contested early pace (from start to first call or farther) and a late challenge (at pre-stretch or stretch calls) that remains undecided for several strides or seconds, but not beyond one-sixteenth of a mile.

The winner was forced to display its competitive spirit and energies both early and late for relatively short undramatic periods. The drama of the late competition persists for five or six seconds and subsides. The winner has beaten off its challengers. Before the shadow of the wire appears, the race has been won.

The early going was not atypically slow or fast. Contending horses kept abreast of the action by running in customary manner before moving into striking position approaching the pre-stretch call. It has been an average race, the familiar processions that practiced handicappers see so repeatedly that they have internalized the competitive dynamics and recognize them instinctively.

Two variations of the typical race are themselves instantly recognizable. In the first, the early pace contest is faster and sustained to the pre-stretch call or top of the stretch, then the winner prevails and draws off.

In the second, the final drive proves conclusive but unexceptional, lasting most of the stretch among several evenly-running late challengers. The winner prevails in the final 50 to 100 yards. The early pace has been moderately competitive at best and often goes uncontested. Instead of sustained early pace, victory is determined by sustained late drive, but in each situation the degrees of speed and power required remain common. The race remains typical. The rating remains 3.

The most competitive races involve sustained multiple challenges early and late, usually in rapid time, and feature all-out hotly contested stretch runs lasting three-sixteenths of a mile or farther. The Unusually Competitive race often involves an exciting late drive of a quarter-mile. A Strongly Competitive race contains the sustained early-late challenges, but the final drive lasts one-eighth mile or thereabouts.

A Noncompetitive race is characterized by no challenge or by a trivial momentary one near the start. It's a wire-to-wire romp that has been otherwise unexceptional.

A Mildly Competitive race features a single, relatively brief challenge, early-middle-late, with the winner presiding readily, as clearly best. The challenge often occurs between the pre-stretch and stretch calls and does not last long. Within a few strides the best horse draws off emphatically or decisively.

The same kind of mild challenge may occur during the early pace contest but will not endure beyond the first call. It may be represented too by a stretch runner passing a tiring frontrunner, meeting little or no resistance in the passing.

The CQ scale intends to assess the intangibles of class. It is concerned with observable expressions of endurance, willingness, determination, and courage. The Unusually Competitive race is rated 5, the Noncompetitive race 1. The extremes of the scale are intended to reflect extraordinary performances of one kind or another. Most performances will therefore fall in between.

To rate the intangibles horses have exhibited, it's safer and far more efficient to consider the race as a whole, not individual performances, as the unit of analysis. This presents a procedural problem. Ultimately, individual horses will be evaluated, not races. To earn the rating deserved by a Strongly Competitive race (4), for example, the runners-up and other close finishers should have taken part in the combat. This is not always so, as when horses benefit strictly from the competitive action of other horses.

Modern speed handicappers have confronted the same problem. Assigning high figures to impressive winners and comparing other finishers to the winners' times, they risk awarding splendid figures to horses that have merely been dragged along or have just picked up the pieces.

The practical remedy invokes a closer personal observation of the competition. Handicappers intend to avoid rating horses in races where they have not been "competitive." Trip handicapping becomes a tool of class handicapping. Experience shapes the rater's ability to discriminate.

A detailed discussion of the CQ Scale and its application will be presented in the following chapter. It provides a taxonomy of familiar racing situations that can be referenced to each point of the rating scale.

Step 3: Calculating Basic Class Ratings

The class-speed points multiplied by the CQ rating yields the basic class ratings. Examine Table 2.

The far right column of the table shows that maidens can earn as many as 35 class points. They can earn as few as 2 points.

A maiden that wins while leading all the way with an adjusted final time five lengths below par gets 2 class-speed points multiplied by a CQ rating of 1, or a class rating of 2.

A maiden that wins in five lengths above par in a race whose CQ has been judged Unusually Competitive (5) gets 7 class-speed points multiplied by 5, a class rating of 35. Quite a distinction.

Grade 1 stakes winners earn as many as 100 points or as few as 12. Classified allowance runners earn as many as 65 points, the highest rating available to nonstakes horses.

The wide range of points allotted within a class category, or

TABLE 2
Class-Speed Points, Class Pars, and
Top Ratings for 8 Levels of Nonclaiming
Competition

*Variations about Par, Class Pars, and
Top Ratings by Class Levels*

Conditions of Eligibility		Par −5	Par −2, 4	Par ±1	Par +2, 4	Par +5	Class Pars	Top Ratings
	Maiden	2	4	5	6	7	15	35
Alw	NW1xMC	3	5	7	8	9	21	45
Alw	NW2xMC	4	6	8	9	10	24	50
Alw	NW3xMC NW4xMC	5	8	9	10	12	27	60
	Clf Alw	6	9	10	12	13	30	65
Stk	Restricted (R) Open	7	10	12	14	16	36	80
Stk	Listed (L) Grade 3	10	12	14	16	18	42	90
Stk	Grade 2 Grade 1	12	14	16	18	20	48	100

class within a class, reflects the heavy reliance of the procedure on the interaction between speed, the intangibles of competitiveness, and the quality of the opposition.

Apparent anomalies in the procedure and resulting ratings represent logical incongruities more than practical problems. That is, they reflect untenable comparisons. Grade 1 winners, for example, that run two lengths slower than par in Noncompetitive races earn just 14 points. Typical maiden winners earn 15 points. Are those maiden graduates classier than Grade 1 winners exiting the slowest, least competitive stakes? Hardly. How to reconcile?

Not only is the comparison not logical, but the practical consideration is tortured. Few Grade 1 stakes are Noncompetitive or even Mildly Competitive. They are instead intensely competitive as a rule and completed in times faster than the stakes pars, which represent all stakes races on the local calendar.

Where Grade 1 races have been Competitive in par or faster, the minimum rating will be 48, greater by lengths than the most impressive maidens and roughly half the point allotment in the rating scheme. In the isolated atypical circumstances wherein the ratings intimate maidens are superior to Grade 1 horses, handicappers simply ignore the ratings and use their brains.

Table 2 also introduces the concept of class pars. These ratings represent performances equivalent to the speed-class pars plus or minus one-fifth second multiplied by the centerpoint (3) of the CQ scale. Class pars represent the expected class ratings for winners at the various conditions of eligibility.

A horse that wins an allowance race, for nonwinners two times other than maiden or claiming, is expected to earn 24 points. The typical open stakes winner should get 36 points.

Notice the class pars are lower than top ratings by more than 50 percent. The method stresses the intangibles of class more than brilliance. Thus races completed in par that have been Strongly Competitive (4) can earn the winners and close runners-up ratings higher than would performances that are faster than par but just Competitive (3).

The weighting has been deliberate. It counters a conventional overemphasis on speed for its own sake, without overstating the case. Times being relatively equal, by this procedure the most competitive horses will always be rated higher.

CLAIMING CLASS

The procedure for rating claiming races depends on the previously remarked proposition that modern claiming horses move up and down in class effectively within well-known price brackets but move about outside of those brackets only with much greater difficulty. Examine Table 3.

The table allots a maximum 50 points up to the $62,500 selling price, which includes 95 percent of the claiming horses in the nation. Those horses can earn precisely half as many class-speed points as are available to nonclaiming horses. Above $62,500 the points and ratings of Table 3 correspond to the classified allowance row of Table 2.

Similarly, class pars and top ratings of the upper portion of

TABLE 3
Class-Speed Points, Class Pars, and
Top Ratings for Claiming Races

Claiming-price Brackets	Par −5	Par −2, 4	Par ±1	Par +2, 4	Par +5	Class Pars	Top Ratings
			Variations about Par, Class Pars, and Top Ratings by Claiming Classes				
$10,000 and Below	0	1	2	3	4	6	20
$12,500–16,000	1	2	3	4	5	9	25
$20,000–25,000	2	4	5	6	7	15	35
$32,000–40,000	3	5	7	8	9	21	45
$50,000–62,500	4	6	8	9	10	24	50
Above $62,500	6	9	10	12	13	30	65

the claiming division correspond to the allowance portion of the nonclaiming division.

Maidens are set equal to $20,000–25,000 claiming competition. Preliminary nonwinners allowance races correspond to the $32,000 and $50,000 claiming brackets.

Practice with the rating procedure should persuade handicappers soon enough that the method's basic ratings correlate well with the way the great majority of races are contested and faciliate comparisons that are tenable and meaningful. The resulting class ratings should not misrepresent the reality grossly or often. When they do, to repeat, the class ratings are best tossed aside as specious or unrealistic, just as inexplicable speed figures are by better speed handicappers. In statistical procedure, it's not only fair play but intelligent adaptation to eliminate extremes and distortions that are unrepresentative. The ratings are meant to mimic reality, not distort it.

Step 4: Adjustment for Beaten Lengths

Winners, runners-up, close finishers, and others that played a part in the competitive dynamics of races will be rated. To rate nonwinners, deduct points for beaten lengths according to the following formula:

Beaten Lengths					*Adjustments*
Ns	Hd	Nk	¼	½	No Change
¾	to	2			−1
2¼	to	3¼			−2
3½	to	4¼			−3
4½	to	5¾			−4
6	to	8			−5
More than 8					−8

The formula is simple to remember. Regardless of beaten lengths, do not deduct more than 8 points from the basic ratings. It makes no sense empirically, as horses beaten badly contribute nothing to the competition in the late stages. As frontrunners or pace-pressing horses, they contributed a fair share earlier. Do not penalize them for lengths lost when the game itself has already been lost.

What is the class rating for a $50,000 claiming horse that has been beaten 2¼ lengths in a Competitive route completed in an adjusted time two lengths faster than par?

It is 25.

Step 5: Adjustment for Shippers

Shippers can be rated by reliance on the ratios of the average purse values (in thousands) at the respective tracks. Table 4 contains the purse value index for all North American racetracks, as published by *Daily Racing Form*. Purse averages have been rounded down to the nearest thousand.

A shipper from Monmouth Park, where the purse value index is 12, to the Meadowlands, purse index of 15, has its class rating at Monmouth reduced by 20 percent, as the ratio of 12 to 15 is .80 and the basic rating multiplied by .80 is a 20 percent reduction.

Comments on the purse value index of *Daily Racing Form* are pertinent. The index considers overnite and stakes purses in combination. Not so long ago the procedure biased the index to favor the leading tracks terrifically, notably in New York

TABLE 4
Abbreviations and Purse Value Index
for North American Tracks

The following table may be used as an adjunct to *Daily Racing Form's* past performance feature of showing the value of allowance race purses. The number following the name of each track (except hunt meets) represents the average net purse value per race (including stakes and overnight races), rounded to the nearest thousand, during the track's 1984 season. A comparison thus can be made of the value of an allowance purse in a horse's current past performances with the average value of all races at that track the preceding season. The purse value index in the track abbreviation table will be changed each year to reflect the values of the previous season. If no purse value index is shown in the following table, the track did not operate a race meeting last year.

AC — (Agua) Caliente, Mexico—9	FP — Fairmount Park, Ill.—4	Pim — Pimlico, Md.—10
Aks — Ak-Sar-Ben, Neb.—10	GBF — *Great Barrington Fair, Mass.—2	PJ — *Park Jefferson, S.D.—1
Alb — Albuquerque, N. Mex — 7	GD — †Galway Downs, Cal.	Pla — *Playfair, Wash.—2
AP — Arlington Park, Ill.—13	GF — *Great Falls, Mont.—1	Pln — Pleasanton, Cal.—9
Aqu — Aqueduct, N.Y.—22	GG — Golden Gate Fields, Cal.—12	PM — Portland Meadows, Ore.—2
ArP — Arapahoe Park, Colo.—3	GP — Gulfstream Park, Fla.—12	Pmf — Portland Meadows Fair, Ore.
AsD — *Assiniboia Downs, Canada—3	Grd — *Greenwood, Canada—10	Pom — *Pomona, Cal.—13
Atl — Atlantic City, N.J.—6	GrP — *Grants Pass, Ore.—1	PP — Pikes Peak Meadows, Colo.—1
Ato — *Atokad Park, Neb.—1	GS — Garden State Park, N.J.	PR — Puerto Rico (El Comandante)
Bel — Belmont Park, N.Y.—26	HaP — *Harbor Park, Wash.—1	Pre — *Prescott Downs, Ariz.—1
Bil — *Billings, Mont.—1	(Formerly Elma, Wash)	Rap — Rapid City, S.D.—1
BM — Bay Meadows, Cal.—12	Haw — Hawthorne, Ill.—11	RD — River Downs, Ohio—6
Bmf — Bay Meadows Fair, Cal.—9	Her — †Heritage Training Facility,	Reb — †Reber Ranch Training Trk,
Bml — Balmoral Park, Ill.—3	Wash.	Wash.
Boi — *Boise, Idaho—1	Hia — Hialeah Park, Fla.—14	Reg — *Regina, Canada—2
Bow — Bowie, Md.—8	Hol — Hollywood Park, Cal.—39	Ril — *Rillito, Ariz—1
BRD — *Blue Ribbon Downs, Okla.—2	HP — *Hazel Park, Mich.—5	Rkm — Rockingham Park, N.H.—5
Cby — Canterbury Downs, Minn.	JnD — *Jefferson Downs, La.—4	Rui — *Ruidoso, N. Mex—4
CD — Churchill Downs, Ky.—10	Jua — Juarez, Mexico—2	SA — Santa Anita Park, Cal.—28
Cda — *Coeur D'Alene, Idaho	Kee — Keeneland, Ky.—18	Sac — Sacramento, Cal.—5
Cen — Centennial Race Track, Colo.	Key — Keystone Race Track, Pa.—8	Sal — *Salem, Ore. (Lone Oak)—1
Cls — *Columbus, Neb.—4	(Now Philadelphia Park)	San — *Sandown Park, Canada—2
Crc — Calder Race Course, Fla.—11	LA — *Los Alamitos, Cal.—10	Sar — *Saratoga, N.Y.—29
CT — *Charles Town, W. Va.—3	LaD — *Louisiana Downs, La.—12	SFe — *Santa Fe, N. Mex.—4
Dar — Darby Downs, Ohio—4	LaM — *La Mesa Park, N. Mex.—2	SJD — San Juan Downs, N. Mex.—1
(Formerly Beulah Race Track)	Lar — Nuevo Laredo, Mexico — 2	SLR — †San Luis Rey Downs, Cal.
DeD — *Delta Downs, La.—3	Lat — Latonia, Ky.—5	Sol — *Solano, Cal.—7
Del — Delaware Park, Del.—1	Lga — Longacres, Wash.—7	Spt — *Sportsman's Park, Ill.—13
Det — Detroit Race Course, Mich.—5	LnN — *Lincoln State Fair, Neb.—3	SR — *Santa Rosa, Cal.—7
Dmr — Del Mar, Cal.—20	Lrl — Laurel Race Course, Md.—9	STC — †Spendthrift Training Center, Ky.
Dmf — Del Mar Fair, Cal.	MD — *Marquis Downs, Canada—2	Stk — Stockton, Cal.—5
Don — †Donida Fm Training Trk, Wash.	Med — Meadowlands, N.J.—15	StP — *Stampede Park, Canada—4
DRS — †Dal Reo Stock Farm, Can.	Mex — *Mexico City, Mexico	Suf — Suffolk Downs, Mass.—6
EIP — Ellis Park, Ky.—5	MF — *Marshfield Fair, Mass.—2	SuD — *Sun Downs, Wash.—1
EnP — †Enoch Park, Canada	Mth — Monmouth Park, N.J.—12	Sun — Sunland Park, N. Mex.—3
EP — *Exhibition Park, Canada—6	NC — †Nursery Course, Can.	Tam — Tampa Bay Downs, Fla.—4
EvD — *Evangeline Downs, La.—3	Nmp— *Northampton, Mass.—2	Tdn — Thistledown, Ohio—6
Fai — †Fair Hill, Md.	NP — *Northlands Park, Canada—5	Tim — *Timonium, Md.—5
FE — Fort Erie, Canada—6	OP — Oaklawn Park, Ark.—14	TuP — Turf Paradise, Ariz.—4
Fer — *Ferndale, Cal.—2	OTC— †Ocala Training Center, Fla.	Wat — Waterford Park, W. Va — 2
FG — Fair Grounds, La—9	Pay — †Payson Park, Fla.	WO — Woodbine, Canada—14
FL — Finger Lakes, N.Y.—5	Pen — Penn National, Pa.—4	Wyo — Wyoming Downs, Wyo.
Fno — Fresno, Cal.—4	Pha — Philadelphia Park, Pa—8	YM — Yakima Meadows, Wash.—1
Fon — *Fonner Park, Neb.—4	(Formerly Keystone Race Track)	

Tracks marked with (*) are less than one mile in circumference.
† Training facility only.

and southern California, where lucrative stakes programs predominate. As noted previously, all major tracks now compete furiously for stables and horses by brandishing superrich stakes events and a lump sum of stakes revenue that has multiplied abundantly. This complicates the earnings comparisons of individual horses, but the purse value index has become a more stable measure of relative racetrack class.

Common sense predicated on experience plays a vital role here too. When New York horses that have shipped to Florida or Arkansas for winter return to the big city, handicappers would be foolish to reduce the winterized ratings by 63 percent, as the adjustment indicates. The horses are not so much changing competitive environments and colors, as returning to home. They can tackle the New York winter horses successfully.

Likewise, when horses at minor tracks on nearby circuits ship to majors in the vicinity, local handicappers best rely on experience to determine whether the recommended adjustment for shippers should apply.

Lately the claiming horses of Longacres, near Seattle, notably three-year-olds, have shipped to Santa Anita and Hollywood Park during fall and have won at customary selling levels or slightly below. The Longacres purse value index is 7 and Santa Anita's is 28. Should the Longacres class ratings be reduced 75 percent? Not a bit.

Experienced handicappers on the West Coast realize the Longacres' three-year-olds have won repeatedly at accustomed claiming prices because they are established claiming-race winners at those prices. Many of the middling three-year-old claiming horses of Santa Anita are running with inflated prices after washing out in the allowances. Their true claiming class remains unknown. For many, the appropriate level will be below the middle range. The well-established, midlevel, hard-knocking claiming horses of Longacres can trounce them, and do, their lower class ratings notwithstanding.

When older claiming horses ship from minor tracks to major tracks, that's different. The older claiming horses at the majors are well established and rugged. The adjustment for shippers applies.

No adjustment for shippers is necessary for claiming races at $8000 to $12,500. Studies of final times have revealed that a $10,000 horse is a $10,000 horse—anywhere. Given the decline in the quality of overnite competition in U.S. racing, the condition is fairly generalized to the $12,500 level. And horses are often entered for $8000 in $10,000 claiming races. The two levels are interchangeable.

Step 6: Adjustment for Low-Priced Claiming Races at Smaller Tracks

Below $8000, claiming-race class barriers become severe. Horses have difficulty moving up successfully. Consistent runners do not move down unless real value has diminished.

To adjust low-level claiming-class ratings at minor tracks, add the purse values (in thousands) to the basic ratings assigned by this book for $10,000 horses and below. If a $6250 plater runs par in a Competitive race having a purse of $5000, add 5 to the basic rating of 6. The class rating becomes 11. Another $6250 claimer that ran the same kind of race for a purse of $4000 would be rated 10. The procedure applies only when rating claiming horses below $10,000.

Recommended Adjustments

A few trusty guidelines protect handicappers from rating errors of the grossest, most misleading kind.

The following apply to claiming races:

1. Improving three-year-olds can move ahead successfully outside of familiar claiming brackets. Unless the horses went wire to wire without challenge, if impressively improving three-year-olds have won by three lengths or more in par or faster or have won in time two lengths faster than today's par, add 6 points.
2. If older horses moving up following "big wins" have

demonstrated back class at today's claiming level or higher, multiply the last race's CQ rating by today's *class par*. Compare that rating with the rating earned in the last race. Use the higher rating.

3. To rate maiden-claiming horses, use the class-speed points assigned to winners at the same selling prices and divide the basic rating by half. If a $32,000 winner would have earned a class rating of 21 for a comparable effort, a maiden-claiming winner at $32,000 gets a 10 (rounded down).

What is the basic class rating of a $20,000 maiden-claiming winner that finishes a length faster than par in a Strongly Competitive race?

It is 10.

What is the basic class rating of a four-year-old former handicap runner which last out won a Competitive sprint at $40,000 in three ticks better than par and is entered today under classified allowance conditions?

It is 30.

In the same race what rating would have been deserved for a winner that was not a former handicap horse?

It is 24.

Class of the Field

The high-rated horse is the class of the field; the best horse today.

If nothing about the early speed, probable pace, track bias, trainer patterns, or body language figures to nullify basic advantages, current form remains essentially intact, and troubled trips do not play havoc with the ratings or outcomes, the class of the field figures to win.

The qualifiers remind handicappers that fully functioning handicapping supersedes automatic reliance on rating methods and the numbers.

Sprint ratings are not interchangeable with route ratings, especially for younger horses. Both experience and not inconsiderable evidence have shown the quality of endurance as measured over distance is best separated out. Versatile horses therefore will sport a pair of class ratings, such as *S30* for sprints and *R22* for routes.

Sprinters do win a fair share of the routes they enter, notably when multiple route winners have been barred, but the converse does not hold. Handicappers can proceed accordingly. At unrelated distances, it's best to bolster class ratings with supporting evidence of the horses' capacity to get the distance comfortably, such as dosage indexes.

The method does not control for the influences of pace. As pace and class are interlocking, the resulting biases can be serious. Two adjustments minimize potential distortions. One is to supplement class ratings with race shapes. If high ratings resulted following a slow early pace, discount the ratings. Another adaptation assembles multiple class ratings and looks at them analytically, in relation to fractional times and the quality of the opposition.

Once handicappers have acquainted themselves with the fundamental procedures and adjustments described in this chapter, their ability to arrive at valuable class ratings depends on utilizing the Competitive Quality Scale intelligently. The trick is to minimize the subjectivity so common to rating scales. The next chapter is intended to help.

6

The Competitive Quality Scale

How might handicappers assess accurately the abstract qualities of thoroughbred performance?

The method promoted here puts the burden on observational skills in association with a taxonomy of racing situations that correspond to a scale of ordered points. In the end the observation skills make the crucial difference, but they develop sharply with practice, as does all skill training. Although experience with trip handicapping no doubt helps, evaluating class looks for intangibles, not position, paths, or trouble spots. The transitions can prove troublesome.

Easy to use procedurally, rating scales come loaded with navigational traps. A few points of departure should steer raters toward a steadier course.

Invoking a scale of ordered points rests on the proposition that horse races are distributed in a normal, predictable manner on the factor to be rated, degrees of competitiveness. Furthermore, the assumption must hold relatively stable across class boundaries.

Fortunately, abundant statistical evidence confirms the case, notably the perfect positive correlation between average final times and class levels. The higher the class, the faster the time. The progression too is standard, of one-fifth or two-fifths seconds. In addition, variations in fractional times surrounding par are roughly the same at all class levels. All types of performances, strong and weak, manage to win at each level, but the central tendencies of the sport do distinguish a lower class of horse from a higher class surprisingly well.

In the present approach the variations about central tendencies—pars and typical degrees of competitiveness—play critical roles in differentiating horses on class. The method features a variation among numerical differences that most rating methods do not. Small numerical differences usually carry the hopes of speed and pace handicappers, making interpretation more difficult. Handicappers will find greater numerical differences here, a function of the CQ Scale. Yet the central tendencies remain sufficiently strong and dominant to prevent matters from getting out of hand.

Consider the shape of the curve in Figure 1. This is called the normal curve. It's a shape of events deeply prized by researchers and statisticians, for it enables them to form gen-

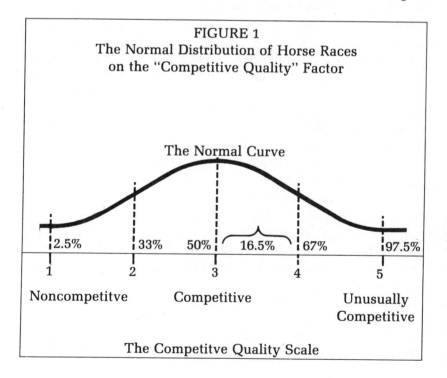

FIGURE 1
The Normal Distribution of Horse Races
on the "Competitive Quality" Factor

The Normal Curve

2.5%   33%   50%   16.5%   67%   97.5%

1   2   3   4   5

Noncompetitve   Competitive   Unusually
                                            Competitive

The Competitve Quality Scale

eralizations about populations (of horses) and to draw comparisons among subgroups (classes of horses) within the populations. It also allows them to draw conclusions about members of similar populations they have not studied directly.

The normal curve plays no less useful a role here. It not only permits the generalization of findings to other major tracks but also illustrates the distribution of horse races on the factor we refer to as *competitive quality*. By understanding the normal curve, handicappers might perform the rating tasks more reliably.

Notice the shape of the curve consists of a wide arc at the center and narrow tails on the ends. This indicates that in any normal distribution of events (horse races) the tendency of the majority is to cluster at the center while only small minorities can be found along the tails.

To the extent horse races are distributed normally on their competitive quality, the majority will cluster near the midpoint of the scale and will be assigned a 2, 3, or 4 rating. Only a small number will fall on the tails and receive a 1 or 5 rating.

It's instructive to realize the actual percentage of races that would be expected to occur at each scale point if thousands of races were rated.

Exactly half would occur at point 3 or below. Another 16.5 percent would fall between point 3 and point 4. Approximately 2.5 percent would occur at the extremes. It's difficult to earn the lowest or highest ratings. Only 1 of 20 races qualifies. They must be unequivocally Noncompetitive or Unusually Competitive. The rating skills of handicappers will be sharpened by appreciating these realities.

Points 2 and 4 on the scale introduce tricky elements of subjectivity. The area between points 3 and 4, for instance, accounts for approximately 16.5 percent of the races. Do the races earn a 3 or 4? It depends. At point 4 some 67 percent of the races have been less competitive. At point 3 half the races have been less competitive. The scale points are continuous, meaning numerous shadings (and ratings) between the two points are plausible. The practical judgment is whether a specific race occurs at a point closer to 3 or 4. Handicappers rely on experience to answer the practical question: has the race at hand been more competitive than two-thirds of all races? Or is it closer to one-half? When in doubt, rate the race 3, as the bias adheres to the center.

The same dilemmas arise when judging races that occur on the spectrum somewhere between points 2 and 1 or 4 and 5. Do they deserve a 2 or 1? A 4 or 5? When vacillating between 1 and 2, assign the 2. Now what does the race deserve when raters feel suspended between points 4 and 5? It rates a 4. Honor the practical imperatives. When in doubt, move toward the center.

Compounding the rater's problem is another element of subjectivity, namely the abstract nature of the factor termed *competitive quality*. What is meant by that? How is competitive quality perceived? How is it assessed as to degrees?

We address the first two questions by considering the several attributes of competitive quality and how horses usually express them in races.

We explore the third by relating numerous operational definitions of competitive races to the five points of the scale.

The remainder of this chapter considers these more concrete definitions of competitive quality, or class.

The Attributes of Competitive Races

The qualities of competitiveness include brilliance (speed), acceleration, willingness, endurance, determination, and courage. To complicate matters terrifically, the qualities are combined to various degrees from race to race, depending to a degree on the instincts and conditioning of individual horses but more importantly on the competitive demands of races at the several points of call.

Naturally, where the competitive challenges have been severe, repetitive, and prolonged, the competitive quality of races will be relatively high. Where race demands have been soft, isolated, and temporary, the competitive quality will be relatively low. Most winners do what is demanded of them; no more. This tendency can complicate the reliability of ratings, a discussion to be taken up in the chapter on interpretation and use.

All of this sounds familiar enough. But how to recognize and rate the several attributes and their interactions during the heat of the race? We begin with operational definitions of the qualities and examples of several.

Brilliance refers to a rate of speed faster than the norm. It is the hallmark of thoroughbred class, particularly when expressed under challenge throughout the late stages of races. The class-speed points of Table 1 assign the highest numbers to the horses that have run the fastest above par. Brilliance owns its own reward. Nonetheless, to create the paradox, few points are awarded to horses exiting brilliantly fast races low on competitiveness, regardless of class levels.

Acceleration is an aspect of brilliance strongly associated with competitiveness. It refers to an intensely improved rate of speed at any point of call when horses have been (a) challenged by other horses for position or (b) sent into a hot pace by the riders.

An accelerating horse is readily spotted by race watchers. The increase in speed is so obvious as to become provocative. The crowd buzzes. What is sometimes less clear are the effects of pace. If the race has been slow, most horses will have been running evenly or decelerating. An apparently accelerating horse may be a mirage. But if the pace has been quick or normal, contending horses will not be easily passed and accelerating horses become notable.

In the usual instance, when challenged, horses simply respond by running faster, either to stay ahead or to keep abreast. The challenge occurs most often between the second and third calls, when horses from behind move up to contest the lead or to gain striking position prior to the stretch run. Horses positioned behind the leaders or in midpack suddenly have been challenged for position or advantage. They sometimes react by accelerating noticeably themselves, to maintain position or to challenge the leaders.

Many times, alternately, contending horses respond instinctively to threats from behind but cannot maintain position, must be pushed hard to keep abreast, or simply fade. This amounts to a notable lack of acceleration, particularly at a point in the race, between late calls, when reserves of speed might reasonably be expected. Mark those horses down.

A trickier matter is whether to credit horses moving ahead and challenging between calls. As noted, horses sent forward to challenge between calls when the pace is slow are not really accelerating. They merely display normal degrees of speed.

The classic situation involves horses situated behind the pace in middle-distance routes that suddenly shoot to the lead approaching the far turn or nearing the middle of the turn. Often the horses are seizing a tactical advantage, not responding to challenge for position or moving into a rapid fractional time. The increased speed remains within normal bounds, not sharply accelerated.

In the Hollywood Park Derby (Grade 1), on turf, in fall 1985, Slew the Dragon seemed to explode between calls on the far turn. The son of Seattle Slew drew out quickly, assuming command by several lengths. The crowd hummed. Yet the acceleration was more delusional than real. The pace had been tardy. Slew the Dragon picked it up and stormed to the front. That nothing chased the colt home had more to do with the lackluster quality of the field than the sudden burst the winner exhibited. Although manner of victory was unmistakably impressive, the race could be rated no better than Competitive (3) and arguably as low as Mildly Competitive (2).

This is a delicate but crucial distinction that handicappers can expect will hound best efforts to rate races on competitive quality, especially in the beginning, and when jazzier horses are involved. Be aware that horses move up or ahead between calls by advancing on slow and ordinary fractions and do not merit extra credit for acceleration. Become strict on the point. Double check the fractional times. Pay attention to the day's variant. Review the replay. Try not to be misled by pace or by the overreaction of the crowd.

Willingness, determination, and *courage* comprise the oft-remarked but poorly comprehended intangibles of class. With practice, much of it, the qualities can be observed and rated reliably. Except in certain instances, however, the intangibles are not readily inferred from the running lines of the past performance tables. This is because the intangibles intermingle on the track with brilliance, acceleration, and endurance, thereby transforming thoroughbred class into a higher order of abstraction than is customarily understood.

These abstractions differentiate class appraisal from aspects of trip handicapping which can be inferred from the running lines. Wide trips from outside posts, the fall-back and come-again patterns, inside and outside biases, positions on the far turn and entering the stretch, getting blocked or taken up, lugging in or bearing out, stumbles at the start—these and other indicators of troubled trips often are revealed in the past performances or result charts. Handicappers have grown accustomed to having the data. But the intangibles of class are not so readily recorded. They often must be witnessed, and witnessed by well-rehearsed observers.

Here are the telltale signs:

Willingness is the readiness with which horses respond to opposition, to mishap, to riders, or to uncertain footing. Classier horses are almost eager to respond to incidents that interfere with the running or to handling that suggests it's time to do your best. Cheaper horses sulk, shy, hesitate, climb, refuse, fall back, or quit.

If horses have been fanned outside of their appropriate lanes, do they continue on aggressively or fall back?

If horses have been forced to wait, to check or steady in traffic, to take up unexpectedly, or to go around, do they respond quickly when clear? Are they instead timid or reluctant?

When horses have been challenged at points of call do they respond immediately by running harder and digging in? Or do they willingly yield the ground?

If horses have been bumped sideways or forced to alter stride abruptly, do they soon regain their composure with the same measures of speed and fighting spirit? Or do they sulk and quit?

If horses have been hard-held in the early running, perhaps

against their will, do they respond generously when finally re-
leased? Or do they spit out the bit and refuse to extend themselves?

In the normal course of the race, when jockeys ask for
greater speed or effort, do they get it, or do horses merely continue to run apace or to fall back?

Handicappers might have less difficulty recognizing willingness if they can appreciate the long-suffering lament of trainers
and jockeys that the very act of horse racing appears foreign to
the thoroughbred's constitution and temperament. That is,
racehorses are naturally unwilling. Few of them appear to
enjoy running to exhaustion in packed quarters across unpre-
dictable obstacles under a stinging whip. The unabashed fighting spirit stands out as counterpoint. When horses do respond
willingly, to challenge or mishap or rider, the cooperation becomes noticeable. Handicappers may not have become accustomed to looking for those kinds of responses—they see first
the trouble—but the observation skills can surely be developed.

An enduring obstacle to proper race-watching, of course, is
the bettor's extraordinary preoccupation with (a) his personal
choice and (b) the talent or willingness of jockeys. If handicappers can suspend disbelief in the competence and motivation
of riders, they can more clearly perceive the willingness or reluctance of horses. Horses that do not want to run faster and
harder than other horses do not become classy horses. It does
not matter how fast they can run. Eventually racehorses begin
to feel tired or extended. Unwilling to extend themselves beyond normal limits, ordinary horses much prefer to stay even,
to fall behind, or to give up. Credit horses that are obviously
generous with natural abilities. It's a strong indicator of class.

Determination means the capacity to sustain a strong competitive response across longer intervals of time and distance. A
willingness to compete, the initial response, persists, under
pressure, for a sixteenth of a mile, an eighth of a mile, a quarter
of a mile, or farther, as long as it takes to quell or overcome the
opposition. Determination becomes noticeable for how long it
persists.

In routine situations a sustained competitive response creates a fight that does not last long. Several strides later the superior horses begin to dominate. The contest has been settled before a sixteenth of a mile has been traveled. The need for obvious determination dissipates.

In more competitive races a severe challenge remains relatively constant and the appropriate response must persevere. In the end the classier horses prevail, but not before fighting stubborn foes into submission. It takes an abnormal time to do the job.

But not always.

The quality of determination can sometimes be observed at early points of call as well as later. Some thoroughbreds, for example, are ferocious out of the gate. The first great horse I ever watched was like that. It was Ack Ack. A front-running monster of the third dimension, Ack Ack simply crushed any horse that attempted to keep abreast of him early. He never once lost that battle.

Once an eastern stakes star traveled west to tangle with Ack Ack in a prestigious Hollywood Park stakes at 1¼ miles. The shipper was a frontrunner too. In a long run to the clubhouse turn the shipper broke sharply and raced slightly in front of Ack Ack from the outside. That spelled its premature doom. Ack Ack just demolished the horse before the two had rounded the first turn. The poor thing finished a ragged last. Ack Ack breezed along when clear to win by open lengths. It was an unequivocal demonstration of top-class determination.

Using this book's procedure I would have rated the race a 4, despite the winner's easy going through the late stages. The real test had come early. Yet it was strongly challenging and determined.

Years later a Cal-bred son of Windy Sands possessed the same upper-class tenacity out of the gate. Eleven Stitches exited at full throttle. In a performance that would have rated 5 on the CQ Scale, Eleven Stitches took the Hollywood Gold Cup of 1981 by beating off several pace-pressing horses before reaching the second call, next staying abreast of new challengers around the far turn and into the stretch, next drawing clear by a determined half-length in the upper stretch, and finally holding at bay a late-charging Temperance Hill to survive by a short head.

Eleven Stitches performed a cut below champion status perhaps, but he was a high-class hombre marked by unbending determination at every point of call. All major circuits boast horses wearing similar stripes. They are roaring tigers from start to finish and not easily defeated.

Regardless, determination is normally expressed in the later stages. Determined horses dig in and run hard with a forward all-out thrust, ears pricked, that remains relentless. The response need not last beyond a sixteenth of a mile to qualify. The fully determined response lasts only as long as it takes. If that means it must persist from the quarter pole to the wire, it does. It might last just a sixteenth, however, or one-eighth. And in numerous situations similar to the Ack Ack example, a first determined response lasts for a sixteenth or so but is taken up anew when other challengers appear later. As will be seen, the duration of the determined response influences the rating a race will receive, but the essence of the attribute concerns instead extending abilities and capacities to meet challenges and toward their natural limits.

Courage can be defined as an exhaustive challenge-and-response pattern sustained beyond the normal limits of physical capacity. Speed and endurance have been exhausted. Determination already has been carried to its extreme. All that is left is the will to win. The horse, as the saying goes, is running strictly on courage; on heart.

While courage deserves the highest competitive value (5) at all times, the quality is not easy to identify. Exactly when have horses' physical resources been depleted? When are they continuing on guts alone?

As a practical guidepost, the final challenge should have begun a quarter mile out or farther. The long, long duel may consist of a head-to-head challenge between two gallant stakes stars, à la Affirmed and Alydar, or of repeated challenges by several horses against a gallant foe, such as tenacious front-runners often encounter, but it is continuous. The winner endures and survives beyond any reasonable physical expectation. It's the ultimate confrontation, demanding the ultimate performance. The performances are given only by the classiest horses at the various levels of the competition.

It's instructive to recall some of the most courageous races of recent times.

The classic demonstration was between Affirmed and Alydar in the Belmont Stakes of 1978. That magnificent confrontation lasted fully six furlongs of the 1½ miles. As combined degrees of speed, endurance, willingness, and determination intensified while the two approached the eighth pole, Alydar momentarily headed his bitter rival. But soon inside the sixteenth pole all physical limits of both three-year-olds were exceeded. Affirmed came on regardless, as relentlessly as ever, to win barely. Affirmed possessed a measure of courage Alydar could not quite match.

Five years earlier in the same classic, Sham, a gold-plated challenger, had attempted similar tactics with the great Secretariat, but the red champion repulsed the challenge in a sixteenth and proceeded to dispense the greatest racing performance on record.

In the 1978 Jockey Club Gold Cup of New York at Belmont Park, in the slop, Exceller and Seattle Slew engaged in the most thrilling stretch run of the decade. Seattle Slew had battled a blistering pace. Exceller had come from 22 lengths behind to catch 'Slew in the upper stretch. Exceller took a half-length lead. Seattle Slew fought back. The two bobbed heads the final sixteenth, both horses exhausted but neither defeated. Exceller won by a short head in as game a finish between a pair of champions as any racing enthusiast will ever see.

In the same Gold Cup of 1979, Affirmed held off a determined Spectacular Bid for five-sixteenths of a mile in the long Belmont stretch. Both champions refused to yield an inch, and Affirmed won again. That resourceful colt became a personification of courage. Once physical limits had been overreached, the advantage belonged to Affirmed.

The remarkable John Henry was the same, but with an interesting twist. John Henry did not possess spectacular reserves of speed and acceleration, but he had tremendous endurance and determination. The longer the race, the better John Henry performed. His physical reserves, endurance absolutely, were not depleted as quickly as other horses'. Moreover, at exactly the moment when natural capacities did run out, John Henry dug in doggedly and continued to run without a trace of deceleration. John Henry might be beaten by better, but never by another horse running out of gas.

I once wagered $500 that a stakes horse named Spence Bay would upset John Henry in the 1½-mile Oak Tree Invitational, on turf, at Santa Anita. At his best Spence Bay had enormous between-calls acceleration. He had shown in his previous start, a minor stakes win, that he was prepared to explode in the Oak Tree Invitational (Grade 1). The public gave me 9–2, second choice to John Henry, an underlay, as usual.

At the quarter pole, with pace-pressing John Henry now drawing away incrementally from the other frontrunners, Spence Bay suddenly took off like a rocket, circling horses with abandon, and nearing the eighth pole he roared past John Henry. John Henry dug in as always and resisted as best he could, but inside the eighth pole Spence Bay had pulled away by three-quarters of a length and was going full of steam. John Henry looked beaten.

Just inside the sixteenth pole, Spence Bay's stamina faltered slightly. He began to tire. With a display of courage like his opponent was certain to mount, Spence Bay could have accomplished the major upset of the season and enhanced his own reputation. He didn't have it. Finished physically as the finish approached, Spence Bay proved unable or unwilling to mount the extra effort he suddenly needed.

John Henry, as all remember fondly, did the opposite. He kept charging, full bore, all the way. The all-time turf champion won, and the final margin proved as wide as a length. John Henry received a standing ovation for the courageous comeback. Spence Bay showed impressive acceleration, all right, but unimpressive courage.

Courage can be seen at all distances at all class levels but is ordinarily observed best in the longer races for better horses. After physical energies have been spent, the classiest horses struggle on. The best horse wins.

Handicappers should not believe unusual demonstrations of courage are necessary to award a competitive quality rating of 5. All races judged Unusually Competitive deserve the 5. The next section connects the attributes of class and the characteristics of races to the five points on the CQ Scale.

Points on the Scale

Moving upward from the low end, handicappers as raters will discover the bottom scale point the easiest to identify on the track. The circumstances are familiar to all.

Point 1. A wire-to-wire romp is a Noncompetitive race. The horses lead uncontested from flag fall to finish. No amounts of willingness, determination, endurance, or acceleration are called into play. Early speed has proved enough. It may be cheap or precious; no one knows. With one exception, the pace and final time remain irrelevant. Uncontested front-running winners are assigned a 1.

The exception is the frontrunner that not only runs fast all the way but *wins with evident reserves of speed and power.* The jockey will be still. Perhaps the horses will be geared down; deliberately slowed. The winner is practically looking for a reason to do more. That horse qualifies for a "projected" rating. So do other kinds of winners. More on this concept at the chapter's end.

Another race that rates a 1 involves the frontrunner's opposite number. This horse wins from far behind, but not through any effort of its own. It wins because battling pacesetters that have been overexerted slowly perish. In the typical situation a surviving frontrunner draws clear while tiring. Sometimes the front end just collapses. Early runners have been fatigued prior to the stretch call or just inside it. Nothing from just behind the pace can grab the advantage. A come-from-behind type runs as evenly or ploddingly as ever, yet wins. Victory is achieved by default. Something has to win. Give the race a 1.

Unlike most contested races, Noncompetitive performances often can be inferred from charts or past performance tables.

They look like this:

Front-running **Cresta Lady**   B. f. 3, by Cresta Rider—Rare Lady, by Ne·
romp: **VALENZUELA P A**   **115** Br.—Mabee Mr-Mrs J C (Cal)
             Own.—Vistas   Tr.—Wheeler Lin
                                                  Lifetime   6   2   0   3 $29,705
             30Apr86-7GG   6f :21⁴ :44¹ 1:09 ft *7-5 114   2½ 21½ 23 34   Diaz A L⁵ ⑤Aw17000 90-16
             11Apr86-1SA   6f :22 :45 1:11²ft   2½ 118   1² 1⁴ 13½ 12½   Stevens G L⁶ⓕ c50000 81-17

             Nick's Prince ∗ ⓒ″   Ch. g. 3, by Elegant Prince—I'm for Maggi
             SIBILLE R ◯-◉ ◠ **114** Br.—Doughrty-Clvlnd-Plescia (Cal)
Late-running Own.—Benon-Fleishman-Levin et al   Tr.—Soriano Morris
chug: Lifetime   10   4   1   4 $52,000
             30Mar86-7SA   1 :46³ 1:12² 1:39³ft 13 116   8¹⁴ 87¹ 43½ 31½   DJhoussyE⁸ ⑤Aw31000 69-24
             15Mar86-9SA   1¹⁄₁₆:46³ 1:12 1:46¹m 10 116   8¹³ 8¹² 34½ 1½   DelahoussayeE⁴ 50000 70-23

In the first instance, the winner will be tired just the same. In the second, the final-quarter time will be tortuously slow, not-withstanding a rapid pace. In fact, where the final quarter has been fast or average, the race deserves better than the lowest rating. The winner was not Noncompetitive.

Point 2. A Mildly Competitive race is characterized by challenges that are fleeting and unimpressive. Any struggle that takes place will be brief. Challenges often occur at the first or second calls. In the stretch they begin and end without suspense. The late challenge is ended within seconds. The horses try, but it's no contest.

Regarding the front-running scenario, now the pace may be contested, but not beyond the first quarter-mile. After gaining an advantage, the frontrunners relax and win handily.

A variation of the race finds a lone frontrunner dashing clear early, without exertion, relaxing between calls, but challenged briefly at the pre-stretch or stretch calls. Within a few undramatic strides either the frontrunner draws off anew or the challenger sails by. Either winner earns a 2.

A second Mildly Competitive race finds the pack racing evenly and tightly bunched during the first calls, after breaking without much combustion or infighting for the early lead. The front flight races abreast, relaxed and rated, while moving along uneventfully in ordinary time. The off-pace horses gather themselves in position behind the front lines and race without provocation or maneuvering. The laggards fall back and wait. A solemn procession is an apt analogy.

The procession continues without incident until the pre-stretch call nears and the jockeying for striking position and advantage begins. When the real competition begins, the suspense does not last long. Within seconds a horse commands the advantage and draws out, continuing to the wire unmolested. Horses and jockeys may be flailing away, but not much of a contest develops. It's just an even race, having a mild undramatic challenge midway and a handy winner late. It rates 2.

When a late-comer wins a Mildly Competitive race, it normally tackles a tiring front-running type near the eighth pole or sixteenth pole. The front horse responds as best it can, but in a few yards the race is decided. The late runner draws clear.

In these situations only a modest amount of willingness and determination has been requisitioned and exhibited. Final times often will be average to slow, but not necessarily. Times swifter than par can result from weak competition, and often do, a weakness of speed handicapping. In numerous cases, an internal fraction or two might reveal authentic outlays of speed but not the race in its entirety. The action has heated only temporarily, until the losers concede and the winners pull away. The action then slows again, about as quickly as it began.

Point 3. A major-league horse race features a contested early pace followed by a late challenge. The early fight lasts a quarter-mile or farther before the struggle temporarily abates.

The salient characteristic of the late challenge is that it lasts approximately one-sixteenth of a mile, perhaps a little longer. Between the three-sixteenths pole and the eighth pole, or between the eighth pole and sixteenth pole, the final battle is waged and decided. Eventually a horse takes an advantage while the others continue to press unsuccessfully.

If the late-comers are picking up stretch ground, either they fall a bit short or arrive in the lick of time. The prolonged battles into deep stretch that might have taken place, changing the colors of the competition, do not materialize for one reason or another, normally because one horse has proved superior. The race has been decided before the shadow of the wire appears.

A challenge early, a challenge late. A late drive undecided for approximately one-sixteenth. Your standard Competitive race. It rates a 3 on the CQ Scale. Several variations of the routine race should register with regulars.

In one, the first flight of runners continue battling with one another into the stretch. Near the eighth pole one draws off and wins. If the pace were slow early, it usually will be average to fast late.

A second common variation of the typical race finds a late-comer chasing a tiring front-end survivor through the lane. The late runner catches up near the sixteenth pole. Resistance is provided. The two compete for several strides before the winner prevails. More often than not, the late-comer's momentum and energy reserves preside. The race is rated 3.

In another scenario two or more late-comers challenge the frontrunners or pace-pressing horses in the upper stretch. The struggle persists among several for a sixteenth or so before the best horse draws clear. It's a 3.

In a common variation of the above, the late-comers arrive at the leaders just as they have begun to collapse. The late-comers are left to battle with one another. For a sixteenth or so they do. Again the best horse takes a sure advantage before the wire is crossed.

Each variation of the Competitive race has the late challenge endure for one-sixteenth or thereabouts. Moderate degrees of willingness and determination must be displayed before the outcome has been secured.

In a more subtle variation of the regular race the late challenge itself begins later, near the sixteenth pole, or just inside, and the combatants persevere until reaching the wire. The finish may be tight, but it remains typical. As a routine brand of competition, it earns just 3.

Point 4. If the average race features an early and late challenge, the latter lasting approximately one-sixteenth, the Strongly Competitive race features (a) repeated serious challenges or (b) an extended dramatic challenge throughout the final eighth-mile or final three-sixteenths.

The early pace is contested hotly for three-eighths or farther, and the late drive is contested strongly for one-eighth or farther.

Race shapes are normally average-fast, fast-fast, or fast-average, but the distinguishing mark is the duration and determination of the struggles for advantage and victory. Both the early and late demands require generous outlays of speed and determination against severe pressure. The winners will have run fast and hard most of the way. So will have several losers.

Winning frontrunners will seem especially notable. They must battle for the lead among equals for three-eighths or longer. They are not racing relaxed, but firing. Eventually they do secure the lead, on the far turn perhaps, and take a breather. But soon they are strongly challenged again, often by off-pace horses that have chased the early pace without experiencing the intense head-to-head combat up front. In the upper stretch or approaching the eighth pole, the final challenge begins. It is severe and persistent. Relatively strong combinations of speed, endurance, and determination have been on display throughout most of the race. Victory has been hard-earned. It often is close. Less than a length, a photo. Invariably, the outcome remains in doubt far inside the sixteenth pole. The finish is therefore dramatic. It carries an impressive visceral force.

Off-pace horses that win Strongly Competitive races do not enjoy an easy canter at any call. They must pursue the early pace vigorously without letup, retaining striking position around the far turn and into the upper stretch. In the stretch they must find renewed energy to challenge the lead and do battle for one-eighth mile or farther.

When late-comers win the Strongly Competitive race they usually must maneuver into a fast fractional time approaching the pre-stretch call or upper stretch. They then straighten themselves for a continuous running battle that will last practically the length of the lane. It takes inordinate determination to win from behind. Halfway between the sixteenth pole and the wire the most determined late runners often gain the advantage and hold the others safe. But they do not breeze in.

In most scenarios the final furlong will be average to fast, not slowing. The races rate a 4.

Point 5. In the Unusually Competitive race the combined qualities of speed, endurance, and determination are extended for a quarter mile or farther. The contending horses are severely tested throughout the late stages, if not all the way. The pace is rapid and contested. The final furlong will be especially difficult and punishing for all concerned. Maximum amounts of energy will be spent unremittingly. The horses become exhausted but press on. The best of the best take one another past natural limits. Occasionally, handicappers notice the horses having difficulty maintaining a straight course, but they do. Jockeys are working at full force and in rhythm with the horses. Finally the most courageous horses overreach the others. They are thought to be running "on courage." It's true. Others falter barely, as stamina cracks, even though willingness and determination do not.

Frontrunners that win Unusually Competitive races can be accepted as the classiest horses on the grounds. They have delivered the maximum combinations of speed, endurance, and determination for the longest durations. The pace has been fast-fast without pause. Pressure has proved relentless. The horses have tired by the stretch call, if not before, but have won regardless. Award the 5.

When off-pace horses or late-comers earn the 5, they normally do so by taking the baton approximately a quarter mile out, after gaining ground against a rapid pace to reach contention. They then persevere full tilt until the end. Determination has been operating for a half mile or more. The final challenge has been all-out. The outcome has remained in doubt until the end or near-end. Across lengthy, dramatic, hotly contested distances and time intervals, the horses have surpassed all normal standards and expectations. The races deserve a 5 and handicappers should know it.

Slower, cheaper horses can earn the 5 by the same gritty resolute displays, although the times will likely be average to slow. Do not mark the horses down because they recorded tardier times. If they have been unusually game, over the required furlongs, give the 5.

A recapitulation of race scenarios and rating points can be found in Table 5. With practice, a season's worth, the scenarios and related expressions of intangibles can be observed reliably on the track.

TABLE 5
Race Scenarios for Each of Five Points on the Competitive Quality Rating Scale

POINT 1. NONCOMPETITIVE

1. A wire-to-wire romp by a lone frontrunner.

2. Without any exertion of its own, merely by running evenly or slowly, an off-pace horse or late-comer catches a tiring leader in deep stretch, passing without resistance to win late.

POINT 2. MILDLY COMPETITIVE

3. The frontrunner draws away from a contested pace after only a quarter mile or sooner, relaxes, and wins unmolested thereafter.

4. An off-pace horse or late-comer catches the leader near the pre-stretch or stretch call, and following a brief challenge and several strides, one horse draws off to win.

5. The pack or several horses run easily and evenly to the far turn or quarter pole before one horse draws out to win without late pressure.

POINT 3. COMPETITIVE

6. Any race having both an early challenge and a late challenge, the late challenge lasting approximately one-sixteenth of a mile.

7. A flight of frontrunners continues to challenge one another into the stretch and by the eighth pole the eventual winner draws clear and survives.

8. A late-comer, off-pace type, or several, chase a tiring frontrunner through the lane, catching up near the sixteenth pole, and winning before the wire.

9. Two or more late-comers challenge the front-running horse or pace-pressing horses in the upper stretch, and in another sixteenth or so the best horse pulls away and wins.

10. Two or more off-pace horses and late-comers arrive at the leaders as they are collapsing and continue to battle one another for a sixteenth or so, until one of them manages to wrestle clear and win.

POINT 4. STRONGLY COMPETITIVE

11. Repeated serious challenges early and late, involving the same or various horses, the late challenge persisting for one-eighth mile or three-sixteenths mile.

12. A strenuous prolonged challenge throughout the stretch, beginning in the upper stretch or at the three-sixteenths pole.

13. Frontrunners are pressured strongly early and for approximately three-eighths, draw clear between second and third calls, and soon are challenged again in the late stages, the last challenge lasting about one-eighth mile.

14. Off-pace horses chase a quick pace while retaining striking position, move up to challenge at the pre-stretch or stretch call, and persevere for one-eighth mile or longer.

TABLE 5 (*continued*)

15. Late-comers move into a contested rapid pace approaching the pre-stretch or stretch call, then run determinedly against other horses for an eighth mile or farther, before winning.

POINT 5. *UNUSUALLY COMPETITIVE*

16. A continuous challenge or repeated series of challenges demanding the ultimate combinations of speed, endurance, and determination extended for a quarter-mile or farther. The winner has been all-out and so have several losers.

17. Frontrunners sustain a fast-fast pace under relentless pressure, winning after a bruising final quarter-mile or repeated challenge. Often all physical energies have been exhausted, the horses competing in the end on courage.

18. After gaining ground against a rapid pace, off-pace horses or late-comers take up the final challenge about one-quarter mile out and persevere at full throttle under pressure until the end, winning closely.

Projection

Where races have been judged Competitive, Mildly Competitive, and Noncompetitive, at times manner of victory will be more impressive than victory itself. The winners have exhibited untapped reserves of speed and energy. They might have done more, if asked. The brilliant frontrunner that wins in hand is the classic situation. The fields the easy winners demolish deserve average-to-weak ratings for competitive quality maybe, but the winners deserve much more respect than that.

If handicappers rate these persuasive winners in line with the opposition they have humbled, they risk obscuring the class rises that win with authority a few weeks later. This happens frequently, notably in the nonclaiming three-year-old division.

A tactical remedy projects a higher order of class for the most convincing of winners. Experience with the CQ Scale suggests the projections should adhere to three guidelines:

1. Genuinely impressive winners of Noncompetitive races should be rated two points higher on the CQ Scale. Instead of 1, award a 3.

2. The same procedure applies in Mildly Competitive races where the winners came from off the pace to blow by and win powerfully in sharp time. Instead of 2, give them a 4.

3. Where races have looked typically Competitive, but the winners stunning, winning with obvious reserves, award the standouts the highest rating, a 5.

In all cases the appropriate projection is of two points, not a single point up the scale. The rationale is simply that the winners looked overwhelmingly superior. If that special dimension is missing or doubtful, give the winner the race's rating only.

Moreover, the conventional "big win," of two–three lengths or more after racing close at the stretch call, does not qualify the winners for a projected rating. Big wins must be accomplished with obvious reserves of speed and power. Many are not, and are not repeated against better.

A peculiar feature of projected ratings is that the winners almost invariably become more transparent on second and third viewings, while watching the replays. The judgment regarding reserves becomes crystal clear. More often than not, the easy win has been routinely competitive, not extraordinary. This circumstance strengthens the credentials of those exceptional horses that win while wanting to do more.

At times the official *Daily Racing Form* chartist notices the same reserves and relays the impressions in the result charts. Ironically, one of the most difficult observation skills for handicappers who are not chartists can be found in the charts, as most demonstrations of superior class cannot.

As with other rating methods of handicapping, once the mechanics have been mastered, the fruits of labor depend upon the intellectual skills of interpretation and use. Thoughtful experience becomes an excellent teacher on this front.

A later chapter presents the lessons on interpretation and use a season's application has contributed. First we consider the evidence of the method's effectiveness, a persuasive discussion that points toward general directions of implementation not entirely anticipated.

7

First Evidence: Santa Anita Park, 1986

The new class ratings were tested for 60 racing days at Santa Anita Park from February 1 until April 21 of 1986. Seven off-track afternoons were excluded.

High-rated horses in claiming, nonclaiming, maiden, and maiden-claiming races were studied. The method typically found three or four claiming plays and two or three nonclaiming plays a day. Flat bets of $2.00 were made on 352 starters.

Results appear in Table 6.

An examination of the table reveals the method worked effectively at both the claiming and nonclaiming levels, but with intriguing variations. In claiming races the win percentage for 57 of 189 starters was a marginal 30 percent, but the dollar return (.67) and average odds on winners (4.6 to 1) were unusually high. The bettor's advantage over the claiming game can be estimated at a powerful 15 percent. The advantage permits high-percentage bets of a bankroll, perhaps 5 or 6 percent.

In nonclaiming races (allowance, classified allowance, and stakes) the win percentage for 36 of 100 starters is strong (.36) but the dollar return (.19) and average odds on winners (2.3 to 1) moderate. The bettor's advantage in nonclaiming races can be estimated at 8 percent. The advantage allows a small percentage bet of the bankroll, perhaps 3 or 2 percent.

TABLE 6
Study of Class Ratings at Santa Anita Park, February 1 through April 21, 1986. Win %, Dollar Profit, ROI, and Average Odds on Winners for Four Classes of Competition.

Level	Days	Starts	Wins	Win%	Bet*	Net	ROI	$Odds	Advantage
Claiming	53	189	57	.30	$384	$258	.67	4.6	.15
Nonclaiming	48	100	36	.36	202	38	.19	2.3	.08
Maiden	24	35	11	.31	70	(8.20)	(.12)	1.8	(.07)
Maiden Claiming	21	28	13	.46	56	60	1.08	3.4	.30

* Refers to $2.00 flat bets. Small discrepancies between number of starts and amounts bet is due to the high class ratings being shared by two horses in each of four races.

The data for maiden and maiden-claiming races proved inconclusive but hypothetical. Small samples resulted from limiting bets to horses that satisfied certain protective rules.

In maiden races, where flashy first starters were entered or trainer data indicated other first starters might be dangerous, no bets were placed. In qualifying races for maidens the high-rated horses won a satisfactory percent (.31), but the average odds on winners (1.8 to 1) resulted in supporting underlays that tossed a 12 percent dollar loss. The bettor faces a disadvantage in maiden races of roughly 7 percent.

The maiden-claiming data are characterized by the provocative win percentage of .46. This throws a dollar profit of 108 percent at average odds on winners of 3.4 to 1. Bets were limited, however, to horses that satisfied either of two criteria:

1. High-rated horses must have been dropping from open maiden competition to maiden-claiming races, or
2. High-rated horses that had previously lost a maiden-claiming race must have earned a class rating at least equal to the class par for the selling price.

High-rated prior losers with ratings below the class par were judged unreliable and passed. First starters were considered unreliable as well, with no exceptions. Clinging to these trusty rules, the bettor's advantage in these awful races soared to 30 percent.

When the claiming and nonclaiming races are combined, Table 7 shows the bettor remains at solid advantage.

	TABLE 7							
	Claiming and Nonclaiming Horses							
	in Combination Having the Highest							
	Class Ratings							
Days	*Starts*	*Wins*	*Win%*	*Bet*	*Net*	*ROI*	*$Odds*	*Advantage*
53	289	93	.33	$586	$296	.50	3.7–1	.18

The win percentage for 93 of 289 starters is .33, a familiar statistic, but the dollar return of 50 cents and average odds on winners of 3.7 to 1 exceed dramatically what the public can expect. Bettors are estimated to hold an 18 percent advantage over the game.

Unfortunately, these data reflect the combined influences of the most positive data of Table 6. It borrows the relatively high win percentage obtained in nonclaiming races and the dollar return and average odds on winners obtained in claiming races. The combined data contain biases that handicappers best separate out. That is, the data of Table 6 are more instructive for the practice of handicapping. More on this in the discussion sections.

The plays, wins, seconds, and dollar amounts of each card included in the study appear in Table 8 for claiming races and Table 9 for nonclaiming races. Notice the method selected 46

	TABLE 8					
	Plays, Wins, 2nds, Bets, and Won-Loss Dollar					
	Amounts on High-Rated Horses in Claiming					
	Races at Santa Anita Park,					
	February 1 to April 21, 1986					
Date	*Plays*	*Wins*	*2nd*	*Bet*	*Won*	*Loss*
April 21	4	2	2	$ 8	$33.00	$4.00
20	4	3	0	8	26.40	2.00
19	3	0	2	6	x	6.00
18	3	2	0	6	3.80	2.00
17	4	1	2	8	3.40	6.00
16	3	0	1	6	x	6.00

TABLE 8 (continued)

Date		Plays	Wins	2nd	Bet	Won	Loss
	13	2	0	1	4	x	4.00
	12	3	3	1	6	15.40	x
	11	2	1	1	4	3.20	2.00
	10	4	1	0	8	12.20	6.00
	9	3	1	0	6	4.00	4.00
	6	4	0	2	8	x	8.00
	5	4	1	1	8	11.80	6.00
	4	4	2	0	8	7.60	4.00
	3	3	2	0	6	11.20	2.00
	2	3	1	1	6	6.00	4.00
March	30	5	1	0	10	10.00	8.00
	29	3	0	1	6	x	6.00
	28	4	1	1	8	3.00	6.00
	27	3	1	0	6	3.20	4.00
	26	2	0	0	4	x	4.00
	23	3	3	0	6	33.60	x
	22	4	3	0	8	25.00	2.00
	21	3	2	0	6	10.40	2.00
	19	5	1	1	10	4.80	8.00
	16	4	2	0	8	5.60	4.00
	15	4	2	2	8	30.60	4.00
	14	4	1	1	8	3.00	6.00
	13	4	1	1	8	29.40	6.00
	12	4	0	1	8	x	8.00
	9	3	1	1	6	7.00	4.00
	8	6	3	2	12	14.80	6.00
	7	3	1	1	6	2.80	4.00
	6	4	1	0	8	10.80	6.00
	5	5	1	1	10	4.20	8.00
	2	3	0	1	6	x	6.00
	1	3	1	0	8	12.00	4.00
February	28	4	0	0	8	x	8.00
	27	2	0	0	4	x	4.00
	26	3	1	0	6	5.80	4.00
	23	2	1	0	4	18.60	2.00
	22	5	2	0	10	16.20	6.00
	16	3	0	1	6	x	6.00

TABLE 8 (continued)

Date		Plays	Wins	2nd	Bet	Won	Loss
	15	4	1	1	8	7.80	6.00
	14	4	1	2	8	8.80	6.00
	13	3	1	0	6	6.40	4.00
	12	4	2	1	8	11.00	4.00
	9	4	0	0	8	x	8.00
	8	5	1	0	10	18.20	8.00
	7	5	1	1	10	4.80	8.00
	6	4	0	0	8	x	8.00
	5	2	0	0	4	x	4.00
	1	3	0	1	6	x	6.00
Totals			57	35			

TABLE 9
Plays, Wins, 2nds, Bets, and Won-Loss Dollar Amounts on High-Rated Horses in Nonclaiming Races at Santa Anita Park, February 1 to April 21, 1986

Date		Plays	Wins	2nd	Bet	Won	Loss
April	21	1	0	0	$2	x	$2.00
	20	0	0	0	0	x	x
	19	2	1	1	4	$ 7.00	2.00
	18	2	2	0	4	4.40	4.00
	17	1	0	0	2	x	2.00
	13	3	1	0	6	1.60	4.00
	12	3	2	0	6	26.00	2.00
	11	1	1	0	2	2.00	x
	10	3	0	1	6	x	6.00
	6	3	1	0	6	3.60	4.00
	5	2	1	0	4	4.40	2.00
	3	2	0	0	4	x	4.00
	2	2	0	0	4	x	4.00
March	30	1	0	1	2	x	2.00
	29	2	0	1	4	x	4.00
	28	2	1	0	4	11.00	2.00
	27	1	1	0	2	4.00	x
	26	3	2	0	6	9.20	2.00

TABLE 9 (continued)

Date		Plays	Wins	2nd	Bet	Won	Loss
	23	3	1	0	6	2.00	4.00
	22	1	0	0	2	x	2.00
	21	2	1	0	4	3.60	2.00
	19	1	0	0	2	x	2.00
	16	3	1	0	6	1.60	4.00
	15	2	1	0	4	0.60	2.00
	14	2	1	0	4	1.00	2.00
	13	2	0	1	4	x	4.00
	12	2	0	0	4	x	4.00
	9	3	0	1	6	x	6.00
	7	3	0	0	6	x	6.00
	6	3	2	0	6	11.20	2.00
	5	2	2	0	4	3.00	x
	2	3	2	0	6	12.80	2.00
	1	3	1	0	6	2.00	4.00
February	28	1	1	0	2	4.40	x
	27	2	1	1	4	15.40	2.00
	26	2	0	1	4	x	2.00
	23	2	1	0	4	3.20	2.00
	22	1	0	1	2	x	2.00
	16	3	1	1	6	10.80	4.00
	15	2	1	0	4	0.60	2.00
	14	1	0	0	2	x	2.00
	13	2	0	0	4	x	4.00
	12	3	0	1	6	x	6.00
	8	1	1	0	2	2.80	x
	7	2	0	0	4	x	4.00
	6	2	0	0	4	x	4.00
	5	3	2	0	6	8.20	2.00
	1	4	3	0	8	8.60	2.00
Totals			36	11			

place horses as well, a win-place rate of 48 percent. Public choices finish first or second roughly 50 percent of the races. The new class ratings perform as well but with the important distinction that they come first or second at significantly higher odds, especially in claiming races.

In sum, the data support the following conclusions:

1. Maiden races excepted, the method of assigning class ratings based on demonstrated ability performs effectively at all levels of the competition at major racetracks.
2. The highest percentage of winners will be found in allowance, classified allowance, and stakes races as a group, but the profits yielded are typical and not sizeable in the short run—a single season.
3. The best dollar return and average odds on winners will be found in claiming races open to older horses.
4. Unusually high seasonal returns are plausible in relation to two situations:
   a. Dropdowns in maiden-claiming races (win percentage)
   b. Overlays in claiming races (dollar return)
5. The method throws an unacceptable rate of loss in maiden races.
6. The second-place finishers in claiming races can be combined with the winners in those races for a win-place rate of roughly 50 percent winners and at odds sufficiently high to key profitable Exacta bets.
7. For long-term investment purposes, three to five seasons, handicappers can win consistently enough in claiming and nonclaiming races combined to show a satisfactory profit and dollar return.
8. The small samples of maiden and maiden-claiming races indicate the data should be considered hypothetical and inconclusive.

Discussion

The evidence suggests the new class ratings will be most useful to handicappers for finding overlays in claiming races. The claim is convenient, as the majority of races at major tracks are claiming races.

The method works satisfactorily in nonclaiming races as

well, but handicappers must be careful here. Underlays in nonclaiming races will be plentiful, and handicappers seeking meaningful seasonal profits must be alert to avoid them. Applications to nonclaiming races and straight wagering should be best for long-term investors. Few recreational handicappers have the patience for that kind of profit seeking.

In claiming races the high-rated horses deserve backing whenever the odds beckon, regardless of point spreads. When the spread in the class ratings is high and the odds delightful, handicappers face situations ripe for a killing. The best opportunity of the season at Santa Anita met those two criteria. It occurred in the 9th race on March 23 and the data looked like this:

Claiming 1 1/16M 4up $40,000 to $35,000.

Contenders	Class Ratings	$Odds
Envious Dancer	20	15
Too Much For T.V.	21	7–2
Knight Skiing	17	7–2
Foreign Legion	25	19
Rajaba	20	4
New Circle	15	18
Tom	22	3
Morwray Boy	22	119
Bedouin	36	10

Bedouin had earned its clearly superior rating against the same caliber ($40,000 claiming horses) three races back, on February 16, when it won by three-quarters in a race that was fast early and fast late. In two starts since, Bedouin had broken slowly against allowance types it could not handle February 26 and had closed considerable ground between calls on turf against $80,000 horses March 7. Now it was being dropped down to familiar $40,000 company.

Class handicappers should have no problem fixing on Bedouin in this middle-distance claiming contest, and Foreign Legion looks second best with 25 points. At the odds the Exacta combinations must be supported, boxing the two top-rated choices and keying Bedouin to other overlays. Handicappers who did that received a splendid return, to be sure, as the result chart testifies. Anyone purchasing multiple tickets on the Exacta box engineered the kind of killing recreational handicappers relentlessly stalk. Profits like these rarely result from a fundamental kind of handicapping. The race qualifies as the method's first shining achievement.

NINTH RACE
Santa Anita
MARCH 23, 1986

$1\frac{1}{16}$ MILES. (1.40⅕) CLAIMING. Purse $27,000. 4-year-olds and upward. Weight, 121 lbs. Non-winners of two races at one mile or over since December 25 allowed 3 lbs.; of such a race since then, 5 lbs. Claiming price $40,000; if for $35,000 allowed 2 lbs. (Claiming and starter races for $32,000 or less not considered.)

Value of race $27,000; value to winner $14,850; second $5,400; third $4,050; fourth $2,025; fifth $675. Mutuel pool $344,216. Exacta Pool $697,158.

Last Raced	Horse	Eqt.	A.	Wt	PP	St	¼	½	¾	Str	Fin	Jockey	Cl'g Pr	Odds $1
7Mar86 $^{5}SA^{8}$	Bedouin	b	5	118	12	11	11½	10½	7½	5½	1½	Hernandez R	40000	10.80
2Mar86 $^{9}SA^{3}$	Foreign Legion	b	5	116	6	4	$5^{1\frac{1}{2}}$	$5^{2\frac{1}{2}}$	$4^{1\frac{1}{2}}$	4^{2}	$2^{2\frac{1}{2}}$	Meza R Q	40000	19.30
27Feb86 $^{7}SA^{3}$	Knight Skiing	b	5	116	5	3	3^{hd}	2^{hd}	2^{hd}	2^{hd}	$3^{2\frac{1}{4}}$	Delahoussaye E	40000	3.60
2Feb86 $^{9}SA^{9}$	Tom		7	116	9	12	$9^{2\frac{1}{2}}$	$9^{1\frac{1}{2}}$	10^{2}	8^{1}	4^{nk}	Valenzuela P A	40000	3.40
23Feb86 $^{9}SA^{4}$	Rajaba	b	6	116	7	5	$4^{1\frac{1}{2}}$	3^{1}	1^{hd}	1^{hd}	5^{nk}	Hawley S	40000	4.30
23Feb86 $^{5}SA^{9}$	Morwray Boy		6	116	10	9	$10^{1\frac{1}{2}}$	11^{hd}	11^{hd}	9^{hd}	6½	Ortega L E	40000	119.60
20Jan86 $^{5}SA^{12}$	Reserve	b	5	116	3	7	6^{hd}	$7^{3\frac{1}{2}}$	6^{1}	7^{hd}	7^{hd}	Kaenel J L	40000	70.10
28Dec85 $^{5}SA^{7}$	Envious Dancer	b	4	117	1	2	2^{hd}	4^{hd}	5^{3}	6^{2}	$8^{1\frac{3}{4}}$	Pincay L Jr	40000	15.50
22Jan86 $^{5}SA^{6}$	Dare You II		8	116	4	8	8½	$8^{2\frac{1}{2}}$	9½	$10^{3\frac{1}{2}}$	9^{nk}	Stevens G L	40000	24.50
14Mar86 $^{7}SA^{1}$	Too Much For T. V.	b	6	118	2	1	1½	1½	3^{1}	3^{hd}	$10^{4\frac{1}{2}}$	Marquez C	40000	3.90
16Feb86 $^{9}SA^{8}$	Allez Britain		6	116	11	10	12	12	12	12	11^{nk}	Olivares F	40000	24.50
5Mar86 $^{9}SA^{4}$	New Circle		6	116	8	6	7^{4}	6^{hd}	8^{hd}	11½	12	Solis A	40000	18.10

OFF AT 5:37. Start good. Won driving. Time, :22⅘, :46⅖, 1:11, 1:37⅕, 1:43⅗ Track fast.

$2 Mutuel Prices:				
	12–BEDOUIN	23.60	11.60	6.60
	6–FOREIGN LEGION		14.60	7.40
	5–KNIGHT SKIING			3.60

$5 EXACTA 12–6 PAID $1,193.50.

Ro. g, by Al Hattab—Lady in Red, by Prince John. Trainer Buonaiuto John. Bred by Elmendorf Farm (Ky).

BEDOUIN, unhurried early, angled over to save some ground, began rallying in earnest after a half, lost ground when forced to come into the stretch five wide and continued closing in the last furlong to run down FOREIGN LEGION near the end. The latter, four wide to the stretch, was climbing early in the run down the backstretch, moved up to take a short lead between calls in the final furlong but could not resist the late charge of the winner. KNIGHT SKIING, wide into the clubhouse turn, battled for the advantage to midstretch, then weakened slightly. TOM lacked early foot, had to alter course in midstretch while rallying and found his best stride too late. RAJABA, five wide into the clubhouse turn and three wide into the far turn while a pace factor, came into the stretch three wide, continued to vie for the lead to midstretch, then weakened. MORWRAY BOY entered the stretch five wide and was going well late. ENVIOUS DANCER, on or close to the pace for six furlongs, gave way. TOO MUCH FOR T. V. battled for command to the final furlong, then also gave way. NEW CIRCLE, in contention early, faltered.

Owners— 1, Rappa Margaret F; 2, M B M Enterprises; 3, K & L Stable; 4, Clear Valley Stables; 5, Chandler & Wynne; 6, Whiteriver Farm; 7, Keck H B Jr; 8, Four D Stable; 9, Rimrock Stable; 10, Cuadra San Diego; 11, Abrams S A; 12, Hagen Jennifer S.

Trainers— 1, Buonaiuto John; 2, Hageman Walter; 3, Stute Warren; 4, Shulman Sanford; 5, Mandella Richard; 6, Goldberg Lore; 7, Whittingham Charles; 8, Fulton John W; 9, Hutchinson Kathy; 10, Ordones Francisco; 11, Palma Hector O; 12, Hagen Jennifer S.

Overweight: Envious Dancer 1 pound.

Too Much For T. V. was claimed by Bronson & Vallone; trainer, Canani Julio C.

Scratched—Mummy's Pleasure (16Mar86 $^{4}SA^{4}$).

The winner represents an especially provocative illustration of the new class-rating method in action. Bedouin began its Santa Anita campaign as a forlorn $20,000 middle-distance claimer January 4, losing twice while dropping in class before winning when lowered to $10,000 on January 17. It then began an amazing ascent, winning five times and eventually beating $50,000 horses and being voted Claiming Horse of the Meeting.

At each succeeding rung on the claiming ladder Bedouin's prior class rating signaled the strong possibility the horse would win again. On March 23 its class edge looked pronounced, and was. The public saw the ambitious step-ups and backed away from the horse. The class ratings supported each class rise. As a result, Bedouin became a consistent overlay, the only horses by which talented handicappers can beat the game.

In this exceptional example, the two highest class ratings finished one-two and keyed an Exacta worth $1,193.50. An obviously superior selection returned $23.60 to win. The rating procedures promoted here are designed to uncover precisely those kinds of hidden opportunities. The lesson is that recreational handicappers benefit most if they rely on the procedures at exactly those opportunistic times. When a well-grounded rating method makes crystal clear to handicappers a situation not so obvious to the public, that represents the short-term power of the method. It provides immediate assistance not available otherwise. Seize the advantage. Trust the method to spot the bargains. Take the odds.

Selections in nonclaiming races win at powerful rates, but the better horses more often become attractive to the crowd as well. The public favors demonstrated class in nonclaiming races and overbets those horses unmercifully. Handicappers have two options. First, insist on the value that higher odds provide and ignore low-priced selections in the straight pools. Second, convert low-priced straight plays to exotic overlays.

I hope handicappers understand that low-priced overlays can benefit them in the long run but do little to bolster short-range profits. A clear appreciation of purpose is important. Do handicappers seek the incremental rewards of long-term wagering with systematic methods that work well enough to give them an edge? Or do they prefer reaping larger values in the short term with outstanding overlays? If handicappers prefer the latter, they must pursue the higher priced selections not obvious to the multitudes.

Maidens have no categorical class, of course, which explains why the class ratings record losses in those races. The most outstanding maidens, based on past performances, become obvious to just about everybody. They therefore race as underlays.

In the present study, which occurred from February through April, maiden races featuring first starters with sizzling workouts and trainers with positive performance data were skipped. This is less necessary later in the year, beginning late spring. Handicappers know that first starters in races for older maidens win significantly fewer than their fair share of the races, a trend that accentuates as the year proceeds. Maidens having the highest class ratings from previous solid performances should do better at that later time. More data are needed, but when high-rated horses and attractive odds combine in the maiden races of summer and fall, handicappers should get some generous winners.

The maiden-claiming contest is a saltier story entirely. These races provide happy hunting grounds for the new class ratings, as illogical as the proposition sounds. Paradoxically, these runners are so devoid of speed and willingness that even a slight advantage in basic skills gets the job done admirably. Class ratings dominate, as speed figures have not. If the high-rated horse is dropping from straight maiden competition or prior maiden-claiming losers have earned a class rating exceeding par for the class, they enjoy a sharp edge. The odds are frequently favorable, as the public frowns on the repulsive past performances that are portrayed in the *Form*.

The present study clearly indicates handicappers at the majors can survive 40 percent of these slow processions by sticking to the trusty rules—and will find good prices in the bargain.

As always, practitioners are advised that local replications of results should precede serious applications with money. The findings attaching to maiden and maiden-claiming races beg for additional evidence. Although claiming and nonclaiming results at Santa Anita should generalize fairly well to tracks where programs feature $10,000 horses and better, successive replications provide the finer estimates of true performance on which long-term planning depends and which long-term reliability demands. Certainly class handicappers at minor tracks should replicate these findings prior to applying them. The study consumes only a season.

Historically, a failing of handicapping rating methods is the negligence their promoters practice in matters of interpretation and use. Modern speed handicapping suffered the shortcoming for years, notably on the calculation of daily track variants, thereby leaving behind thousands of would-be speed handicappers who did not learn enough to apply the methods or remained steadfastly suspicious of numerical differences of a point or two or three.

Rating methods are hounded too by procedural problems not anticipated on the drawing board. Making sense of the raw materials in practical contexts makes a ringing difference in the results. Experience becomes the best teacher, all right, but only a thoughtful studied experience that best originates with the leading proponents.

The next chapter is intended to afford handicappers a head start with some of the trickier aspects of evaluating thoroughbred class numerically.

8

Interpretation and Use

Rating methods are systematic but not mechanical. They allow room for personal discretion and judgment. Procedural guidelines notwithstanding, individual differences abound, and these influence both the activities and the results of raters. No one should expect therefore that handicappers who use the same rating method will produce the same ratings. They will not. The test is whether the high-middling-low ratings among individual raters correlate well enough to qualify the method as systematic, as opposed to random, quirky, or unreliable.

Experience with the rating procedures tells the tale. It informs users of the obstacles to be circumvented, the pratfalls to avoid. The purpose is to identify the major problems that are recurring so that errors of the grossest kind can be eliminated and individual differences reduced.

The method promoted here results in gross variations among several ratings. The major source of the wide swings is the CQ Scale. Examine the past-performance table below and look at the class ratings Arbitrate earned in its latest two races. The situation illustrates perhaps the biggest headache for class handicappers when first they use the new method.

Class Ratings

Apr 9 S27 (4)
Mar 27 S10 (2)

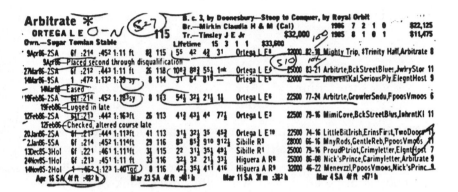

Handicappers will regularly rely on multiple ratings to select a best estimate of true class. On April 9 Arbitrate earned a rating of 27 in a sprint (S) after a Strongly Competitive race, as indicated by the numeral 4. It got just a 10 March 27, following a Mildly Competitive sprint (2).

Which rating is more reliable? The 27 is more representative. It was gained in a competitive race. Less competitive performances deliver less reliable ratings.

The first and foremost bylaw of implementing the rating method therefore concentrates on significantly disparate ratings attaching to competitive and uncompetitive performances. Whenever possible, compare horses by using ratings obtained in competitive races. The CQ Scale ratings will be 3, 4, or 5. Rely on those as best estimates of true performance.

To do otherwise is to risk rating a horse 10 when its best recent effort is closer to 27. By this method, Noncompetitive and Mildly Competitive races penalize horses with significantly lower ratings. That is deliberate. Handicappers want to know what horses can do when they are tested. Races lacking in competitive quality are too often overrated, the winners overblown.

To extrapolate from the above example, the claiming sprinter Arbitrate raced at Santa Anita the day before closing,

April 20, at six furlongs versus $32,000 platers. The three high-rated horses looked like this:

Horses	Class Ratings		Claiming levels
Arbitrate	Apr 9	27	$32,000
	Mar 27	10	25,000
Miami Cove	Apr 5	24	$25,000
	Feb 12	15	25,000
Back Street Blues	Apr 5	23	$25,000
	Mar 27	10	25,000

Rating spreads of three–four points can be decisive, especially when the high rating has been earned against the most advanced competition. These three horses rated close at the $25,000 claiming level, and Arbitrate nosed Back Street Blues March 27 only because that frontrunner burned itself short on the lead and collapsed. Without the April 9 rating versus $32,000 horses, Arbitrate could not be picked against either contender. Its Mildly Competitive figure March 27 would have knocked it down.

Arbitrate won April 20 at 6 to 1, paid $14.20. Miami Cove finished third, ruining Exacta bets.

Several lessons should be stressed:

1. Use multiple ratings, two or three, and analyze each in relation to the facts at hand. Do not sum.
2. Discount ratings obtained by also-rans in races low on competitive quality, unless those are the only ratings available or the best in the horse's record.
3. Credit the most recent rating that is representative.
4. If recent races are not representative (trips, biases, return from layoff, etc.), credit the best recent rating against the most advanced competition.

The Easy Winners. Germane to the above discussion is the carefulness handicappers must exercise in rating the performances of easy winners. The method discounts performances that appear uncompetitive but the winners might have plenty in reserve. Do not penalize them unfairly. The projection technique controls for these paradoxical situations. A maiden that wins wire to wire in par time earns 5 or 15 points, depending on manner of victory.

Did the horse win with lots in reserve? If so, its competitive rating is projected to 3. During the Santa Anita season I found myself changing initial low ratings for approximately a dozen performances. The changes resulted from second and third viewings.

A tactic that controls well for this type of rating error demands that handicappers watch the replay again whenever they assign races a CQ Scale rating of 1 or 2. Focus on the winner. If the manner of victory were powerful, with speed in reserve, mark the performance two points up on the scale. These occasions do not become commonplace, as most horses win straight or fully extended, but they do occur a few times a week.

The Standard Distribution of Class Points. The method has been designed to distinguish the top-class horses at each level of competition from the others. Of the 100 points allotted, handicappers should understand the great majority of races will be susceptible to one-half or less of the possible points. No claiming horse can earn more than 65 points, few earn as many as 50, and few nonclaiming horses earn more than that.

Table 10 shows the top ratings assigned to winners at fourteen competitive levels during Santa Anita 1986. To the right of the eligibility conditions are the class pars and the highest ratings allotted to each level. At the far right are the percentages of points accumulated by winners giving the best performances at each level.

By small increments, notice that the top ratings become higher as the conditions of eligibility become tougher. As the top ratings for the nonwinners allowance series indicate, handicappers confront considerable overlap among closely related class levels. Only in the stakes division do the best horses sort themselves unmistakably on relative class. This mimics reality nicely.

TABLE 10
Top-Rated Horses at Santa Anita Park
1986 by Competitive Levels

Eligibility Conditions	Expected Ratings Pars-Tops	Actual Ratings	Horses	% of Points Assigned
Maiden	15–35	30	Affection Affirmed	.85
		25	Zabaleta	.70
Alw NW1xMC	21–45	40	Comparability	.88
		40	Winter Treasure	.88
Alw NW2xMC	24–50	40	Certainly Super	.80
		40	Nature's Way	.80
Alw NW3xMC	27–60	48	Ice Stealer	.80
		40	Kinda Beau	.67
Clf Alw	30–65	60	Alphabatim	.92
Restricted Stk	36–80	60	Outstandingly	.75
Open		56	Fast Account	.70
Listed Stk	42–90	90	Estate	1
Grade 3		60	Halo Folks	.67
Grade 2 Stk	48–100	100	Precisionist and Greinton	1
Grade 1		72	Hidden Light	.72
		64	Greinton	.64
		64	Ferdinand and Variety Road	.64
$10,000 Clm	6–20	12	Gold Assayer	.60
$12,500–16,000 Clm	9–25	20	Ed's Fantasy	.80
		20	Cold	.80
$20,000–25,000 Clm	15–35	30	Good Thought Willy	.85
		24	Ed's Fantasy	.71
$32,000–40,000 Clm	21–45	40	Indian Flower	.89
		36	Bedouin	.80
		35	National Energy	.79
$50,000–62,500 Clm	24–50	48	Hawkley	.98
		47	Rising Chum	.97
Above $62,500	30–65	50	Honor Medal	.77
		50	River of Kings	.77

Admirably, the method pinpointed Precisionist and Greinton as tops in the older handicap division and Hidden Light and Ferdinand as best in the three-year-old divisions. These ratings were strongly correlated, of course, by other indicators of class and by later performances outside of Santa Anita, notably Ferdinand's at Churchill Downs the first Saturday of May. The method passed a critical test of its merits as events came to pass.

And what of Snow Chief, widely recognized by conventional opinion as the leader of the three-year-old colts at Santa Anita 1986 and the eventual Kentucky Derby favorite?

The method again worked superbly. In the Santa Anita Derby (Grade 1), Snow Chief won off by six lengths as the 2–5 choice, but the adjusted time proved average, the CQ Scale rating 2, and Snow Chief earned just 36 points.

Shouldn't the race's CQ rating have been "projected" to 4, the easy winner cruising in by six? Not at all. Snow Chief had drifted out two lanes while running hard and uncontested. The colt was doing its best, with little in reserve, and the outcome looked better than it was.

In its only previous race at Santa Anita, the California Breeders Championship, a stakes limited to state-breds, Snow Chief had earned just 30 class points while winning by four in a slow adjusted time. Snow Chief became an overrated horse prior to the classics. At underlay odds, it could be dismissed. The class-rating method recognized that. It was the method's second shining achievement.

Notice the top-rated horse at each level normally earned from 70 to 80 percent of the point totals. To obtain 90 percent of the points, races and winners must be fast and competitive. Routinely, races that are Strongly Competitive will record average times. The fastest races just as often will be typical as to competitive quality. The new method is designed to capture precisely these dualities.

Finally, the top ratings at various levels indicate the comparisons among claiming and nonclaiming races that are tenable. Handicappers at major tracks can tolerate the following comparisons well enough to cope:

1. Maidens compare well with $20,000–25,000 claiming horses.
2. Numerous nonwinners allowance competitors can be compared favorably with $32,000–40,000 claiming horses.

3. Classified allowance horses can be compared favorably with $62,500 claiming horses and better.
4. Classified horses compare favorably as well to many restricted and open stakes horse.

Less logical comparisons, such as nonwinners allowance types and open stakes horses or high-priced claiming horses and listed stakes horses, should not be entertained unless exceptional circumstances are well understood.

Back Class. When claiming horses flash sudden dramatic improvement against a brand of opposition they formerly might have pickled, handicappers can prefer ratings attached to "back class" over the more recent lower ratings. The preference finds overlays that figure.

Consider the following data for horses entered for $25,000 in a claiming sprint at Santa Anita on closing day:

Horses	Recent Class	Rating	Back Class & Rating
Speedy	$32,000	16	Not applicable
Bold Topsider	16,000	12	Not applicable
Timlin	32,000	18	Not applicable
Reinbow's Cup	25,000	13	$40,000 27
Tough Enjoleur	20,000	16	Not applicable
Yukon's Star	30,000	17	Not applicable
Woods Lake	50,000	21	Not applicable
Shantin	18,000	16	Not applicable

In its prior start, Reinbow's Cup suddenly stayed close to a rapid early pace and finished a much-improved fourth of 12, after losing miserably versus similar in its previous three. On January 25, it was beaten three-quarters by $40,000 horses, earning the 27 class points that would be sufficient to handle its April 21 field at 13 to 1.

Handicappers might have chosen to pass the opportunity, as I did, because Reinbow's Cup's trainer was roughly 0 for 50 starts throughout the season, but that's another story line. The improving Reinbow's Cup figured on back class following a much-improved performance, had the top figure, and won.

All Below Par. At times all the horses will carry ratings below the class par for today's level. Handicappers should lean on other procedures and discount the class ratings.

The class par for maidens is 15. The following lineup appeared in the sixth, April 18, at six furlongs:

Horses	Class Ratings
On The Close	8
Mastery	8
Members	13
	9
Not The Regular	6

Five other horses in the field had no prior ratings. At a glance Members seems a cinch on class. Each of its two ratings is higher than any other in the race. Eureka! a double-advantage horse.

Don't believe it! Members' highest rating of 13 remains two lengths slower than what has been typical for the class. The horse is not dependable. It did not win April 18. In its second start, following a wide debut March 21 and sparkling workouts since, Mastery torpedoed this mediocre group by seven lengths. Careful reliable interpretation of the numbers saves money and prevents headaches in these matters, where no horses present credentials classy enough to be called the class of the field.

No Contribution to High Rating. A sticky kind of clear-headed interpretation involves high-rated horses that did little or nothing to deserve the ratings.

To recall, the method subtracts from the winner's rating a maximum 8 points for beaten lengths. Check the recent races of the horse below and examine the class ratings for the first race, April 11, a six-furlong sprint for three-year-old fillies, entered to be claimed for $50,000–45,000.

On March 26, Ruffles N Beaus engaged in one of the fastest, most competitive nonwinners allowance sprints of the Santa Anita season. Beaten 10 lengths while 7th of 9, it earned 32

1st Santa Anita *P45²– 111   CP 24-50*

6 FURLONGS
SANTA ANITA

6 FURLONGS. (1.07⅗) CLAIMING. Purse $21,000. Fillies. 3–year–olds. Weight, 121 lbs. Non–winners of two races since February 15 allowed 3 lbs.; of a race since then, 5 lbs. Claiming price $50,000; if entered for $45,000, allowed 2 lbs. (Races when entered for $40,000 or less not considered.) *C3r*

Ruffles N Beaus							Ch. f. 3, by Beau's Eagle—Ruffles N Ribbons, by Olympiad King				
SOLIS A *O–O*			**116**				Br.—Relatively Stable (Cal)		1986	4 0 1 1	$10,850
Own.—Ten Star Stable							Tr.—Lewis Craig A $50,000		1985	4 1 0 1	$15,300
							Lifetime 8 1 1 2 $26,150				
26Mar86-1SA	6f :21² :44² 1:10 ft	12 117	6⁷ 7⁹ 79½ 7¹⁰	Pincay L r⁸ ⑤Aw28000 78-17	Comprblty,FshonDynsty,SDoubyRn 9
12Mar86-3SA	1 :46⁴ 1:12² 1:39¹sy *7-5 110⁵	2½ 2ʰᵈ 1ʰᵈ 21½	Black C A⁴ ⑤c40000 71-25	OurLutka,RufflesNBeaus,Velveteen 7
21Feb86-7SA	1 :47³ 1:12² 1:38 gd 9 108⁵	1ʰᵈ 31½ 3³ 37½	Black C A² ⑥Aw30000 71-22	L7sJoy,Roberto'sKey,RufflesNBus 6
21Feb86—Lugged out early					*AA 112 137' C3-16*
12Jan86-2SA	1 :46 1:11² 1:37⁴ft	33 111⁵	9¹² 8⁹ 55¾ 44½	Black C A⁹ ⑥Aw26000 74-11	Symbolicly,ViolinMelody,Exubrncy 9
12Jan86—Stumbled badly start; very wide into stretch					
5Dec85-8Hol	6f :22⁷ :45³ 1:10¹ft	21 120	55½ 68½ 57½ 513½	Solis A⁵ ⑥Aw20000 80-11	Al'sHelen,AnEmprss,FiryGodmothr 7
22Nov85-8Hol	6f :22 :45¹ 1:09²ft	30 118	6⁹ 58½ 47½ 47½	Solis A⁴ ⑥Aw20000 89-10	T.V.Residul,Erl'sVlentine,TopCorsg 6
2Nov85-12SA	6f :22² :46 1:11¹ft	4½ 117	1¼ 1ʰᵈ 2ʰᵈ 1ʰᵈ	Sibille R³ ⑥SMdn 82-13	RufflesNBeus,Flmboyncy,Sh'sATint 6
23Oct85-6SA	6f :21³ :45² 1:11 ft	19 117	5⁷ 57½ 32½ 3⁶	Sibille R⁷ ⑥SMdn 77-25	T.V.Rstdul,Flmboyncy,Ruff'sNBus 12
23Oct85—Checked at 3/8					
Mar 20 SA 4f ft :50² h		Feb 20 SA 4f m :51 h			

class points, as the winner got a 40. On March 12 at a mile versus $40,000 claimers, Ruffles N Beaus earned an R15.

Here's how the main competition spread itself out April 11:

Horses	*Class Ratings*
Ruffles N Beaus	32
	R15
Exuberancy	26
Queens Love Roses	27
Wine Girl	23
Cresta Lady	27

How to evaluate Ruffles N Beaus?

Regardless of finish, if a horse contributed to the competitive
quality of its race, it deserves the race's rating. Review Ruffles
N Beaus' most recent race again. It plainly contributed nothing,
neither early nor late. In situations like this, class ratings are
easily inflated, especially if the race has been quick and con-
tentious. Prefer instead the most representative recent race at
the distance, which does not help in this instance, Ruffles N
Beaus having routed exclusively earlier in the season.

Class handicappers might have chosen to support Ruffles N
Beaus anyway at 8 to 1 April 11, but the filly finished a well-
beaten second to Cresta Lady.

Double-Advantage Horses. Probability data show unmistakably that horses whose two top speed ratings exceed each rating of the other horses win roughly 275 percent their fair share of the races. Double-advantage horses, as they're labeled, hold a tremendous advantage. The sizeable advantages are sometimes well hidden and the horses pay fair to generous mutuels. The same argument extends conveniently to numerical class ratings.

An obvious double-advantage horse entered the 6th, March 30, a maiden sprint at seven furlongs. The other contenders had started just once.

Horses	Class Ratings
Glimmering Native	11
Kenai Dancer	12
Cheapskate	7
El Corazon	31
	16
Sir Tyson	8
	3

El Corazon had raced eight times, finished second four times, third once. Handicappers traditionally toss these kind away as sucker bait, but the occasional exception is not well understood. If a three-year-old maiden's best races by far have occurred recently, it may be changing colors. El Corazon's rating of 31 was earned by its finishing third in the open Baldwin Stakes, purse of $60,000-added. Its prior maiden figure of 16 had been its best so far easily.

El Corazon won handily; paid $7.80.

Classic Distances. The handicapper's desire to separate the classiest horses in the best races introduces the problem of rating races at 1¼ miles and farther. No par times exist, rendering variations about par moot and the method inoperative. The solution: add 25 seconds to the mile par for the class.

The Santa Anita Handicap, now a million-dollar handicap, occurs at 1¼ miles, as do several of the most definitive stakes on the American calendar. The stakes par for a mile at Santa Anita is 1:35 1/5 seconds. Adding 25 seconds, the 1¼M par for stakes horses is set at 2:00 1/5.

While Precisionist faltered badly, Greinton ran down the 157-to-1 longshot Herat to win the 1986 Santa Anita Handicap in two minutes flat. The route variant for the card, however, was FAST 3. The adjusted time of 2:00 3/5 seconds translates to SLOW 2 about par. The race received a CQ rating of 4.

What is Greinton's class rating?

It is 56.

By this procedure, races at 1¼ miles will yield lower ratings for all but the outstanding distance stars. To interpret the ratings properly, discount classic ratings when generalizing to middle-distance races. Prefer ratings earned at middle distances instead.

For the few races carded at 1½ miles or 1⅜ miles, use the 1¼-mile ratings and emphasize stamina beyond that. In rating the marathons, use the 1¼M fractional time and the procedure described above.

The Cold Exacta. Whenever two horses sport class ratings clearly superior to the rest of the field, they represent an automatic Exacta box—assuming, that is, handicappers find overlay prices on the monitors.

Below are the class ratings for the entrants in the 9th, April 2, at 1¹⁄₁₆ miles for older $16,000 platers.

Horses	Class Ratings
Sir Star	20
Certain Treat	10
Tuscan Knight	6
Creon	25
Frivolissimo	7
Irish Cast	8
Billiken	5
Shuttle Trip	10
Hatamoto	11

Horses	Class Ratings
Navegante	10
Jolly Josh	9
Backlog	6

The race was run to order. Creon (3–1) overcame tons of trouble to finish second. Sir Star (6–1) won clearly. The $5 Exacta paid $147.50, and class handicappers could not have missed it. As in the example, the cold Exactas often materialize in cheaper claiming routes, where many of the entrants have performed pitiably.

The Huge Class Drop. When claimers plunge 50 percent or more in selling price, handicappers must decide whether the horses remain amble enough to win. Obviously, something physical has gone awry. Usually, the end is near. But can the dropdowns survive today?

If three circumstances coexist, handicappers must respect the horses: (a) acceptable odds; (b) signs of life in recent races and workouts; and (c) the highest class rating in the field, provided it exceeds the class par for today's level.

The last condition emerges from the Santa Anita experience. It happens most frequently near the lower end of the claiming ladder, where mediocre horses gather. Trainer Mike Mitchell is known by southern Californians to miss more frequently when dropping and not raising claimers, but on March 13 at Santa Anita 1986 he dropped a plug he had claimed only five weeks ago from $20,000 to $12,500 and selected leading rider Gary Stevens. Lucky Room had been mauled by 21 lengths in its $20,000 try, its second race this year, after staying close enough for four furlongs.

The claiming class par for $12,500 horses is 9. The day's competition, such as it was, sized up like so:

Horses	Class Ratings
Shantin	5
Fortieth Prince	8

Horses	*Class Ratings*
Pickwick Landing	8
Chucklecator	7
Spar Around	6
Lucky Room	10

No other horse matched the class par of 9. At its worst, Lucky Room rated 10, and the horse had worked out sharply twice since its latest dismal yet slightly improved performance. Class handicappers might have decided to key Lucky Room in $2 Exacta boxes with three, four, or five of the others. Exacta projections for Santa Anita's brand-new, first-race, two-dollar Exacta revealed a surprising array of overlays coupled with Lucky Room.

When Lucky Room (14–1) won and Pickwick Landing (12–1) finished second, the $2 Exacta paid $318.50. Multiple Exacta tickets on the combination added up sweetly.

Class dropdowns in claiming races win twice their fair share, and 30 percent drops historically have won 350 percent the races they should. That statistic has dropped but cannot be discarded. Handicappers having numerical class ratings will be better prepared than before to exploit the opportunities.

The Maiden-Claiming Prospects. Whenever maiden-claiming plodders earn a rating superior to the class par for straight maiden races (15), the horses move up instantly as potential bets.

***Nathan** B. h. 5, by Thatch—Glencara, by Sallust
TORO F 118 Br.—Burkhardt & Bellingham (Ire) 1986 2 M 1 0 $3,900
Own.—Duggan–Finucane–Paschall Tr.—Fanning Jerry $45,000 1985 11 M 4 0 $7,808
Lifetime 18 0 5 1 $11,917 Turf 14 0 2 1 $2,362
13Feb86-6SA 1 :46¹ 1:10³ 1:35³ft 3/4 118 4³ 42 1/2 22 1/2 2³ Toro F⁴ M45000 87-14 Carajas, Nathan, Rob This 9
13Feb86—Bumped break; rank early
16Jan86-6SA 1 1/16 :47 1:11 1:42¹ft 12 120 86 3/4 7⁵ 5⁵ 58 1/2 Toro F² Mdn 81-15 Wassl Dancer, Tori's Daddy, Andor 12
29Dec85-1BM 1 1/16 :47 1:11⁴ 1:44⁴ft *2-5 120 2¹ 21 1/2 2¹ 22 1/2 Baze R A³ Mdn 65-22 Silver Top, Nathan, Rapid Act 7
15Dec85-4BM 1 1/16 :47³ 1:12² 1:44³ft *1 122 32 1/2 42 1/4 32 1/2 2² Judice J C¹ Mdn 67-20 Wealthy Dancer, Nathan, RapidAct 8
15Dec85—Crowded at 1/4
7Nov85-8SA a6 1/2f (T):21⁴ :44⁴ 1:15⁴fm 20 118 86 1/4 79 3/4 6⁹ 66 1/4 Ward W A⁶ Aw25000 74-20 CountGeiger, MyGallntGme, QuipStr 9
7Nov85—Lugged in stretch
26Oct85-7BM a1 1/8 (T) 1:48¹fm 27 115 8⁷ 88 1/4 75 1/4 5⁶ Winland W M⁹ 50000 101 — DiplomtRuler, ExcessProfit, RfuldII 11
7Aug85 ♦ 4PhoenixPk(Ire) 1 1/8 2:00¹gd 6-5 131 (T) 2⁴ CrrnG ChrsSmthBldstckPl Side Chapel, Nathan, ‡Napier 4
30Jly85 ♦ 4Galway(Ire) a1 1/16 1:46⁴gd 12 129 (T) — CurrnG McDonoghH BonnieBss, MissNoor, AltosDChvon 17
30Jly85—Left at start. Took no part in race
23Jun85 ♦ 5Curragh(Ire) a6 1/4f 1:14⁴gd 3 1/2 117 (T) 76 1/2 CchrR MdsmmrScryH RngoonRudy, Bllylummin, ErinsStr 20
25May85 ♦ 5Curragh(Ire) 6f 1:19⁴yl 12 121 (T) 2nk CochrnR HrbrtLdgeH Sharp Roi, Nathan, Plum Pie 14
Mar 3 SA 6f ft 1:15¹ h Feb 8 SA 6f ft 1:15⁴ h Feb 2 SA 4f m :49¹ h Jan 18 SA 5f ft 1:01 h

Look at Nathan's recent two races. It was entered March 12 in the same kind of $50,000 maiden-claiming route it lost while placing February 13. How to evaluate?

A much-neglected mistake handicappers repeat ad nauseam is forgiving maiden-claiming losses because of trips. The horses repeat the problems they suffer, so forget it! But if the trouble has been pronounced enough to warrant chart comment, represents an isolated case, and is followed by a solid performance, the occasional exception makes sense.

Nathan is that kind of exception. Not only should the horse have succeeded when dropped into the claimer February 13, its class rating January 16 was 18, three points above par for the maiden class. The winner earned a 26 rating in a strong effort. Its opposition March 12 could not approach Nathan's rating. Horses possessing even hints of authentic ability enjoy a decisive edge in numerous maiden-claiming affairs.

Nathan won—by a nose. It paid $6.60, no great larceny. But the point of the discussion is much larger than the mutuel and will lead to fancier prices several times a season.

The Developing Three-Year-Olds. As many readers no doubt know, one of my favorite topics in handicapping is the developing three-year-olds and how poorly even practiced handicappers comprehend them. Using whatever methods they prefer, all handicappers are invited to try their skill at the past performances on pages 126–128. The new method of evaluating class picks the winner by crediting the best rating three-year-olds have so far managed against the toughest competition they have so far faced.

The eventual winner is actually a stickout, at generous odds, but I believe not one handicapper in twenty can locate it. Examine the horses in the restricted Charles Whittingham Stakes, carded on Santa Anita's unique downhill turf course, and do your best with the data at hand.

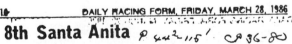

1♦   **DAILY RACING FORM, FRIDAY, MARCH 28, 1986**

8th Santa Anita ρ ₄ₐₐ²₁₁₅'   cρ 36-80

ABOUT 6 ½ FURLONGS. (Turf). (1.11⅘) 2nd Running of THE CHARLES WHITTINGHAM STAKES. $42,000 added. 3-year-olds which are non-winners of a sweepstakes since December 25. (Allowance) Weight, 121 lbs. Non-winners of a race of $20,000 any time allowed 3 lbs.; of $15,000 since December 25, 5 lbs.; of such a race since October 1 or $13,000 since December 25, lbs. Closed 11:00 a.m. Tuesday, March 25 at $50 each with 16 nominations. (Claiming races not considered.)

Smokey Orbit — Ch. g. 3, by Orbit Dancer—Smokey Rae, by Dodger Blue
KAENEL J L — 114 — Br.—Porter K (Ky) — Tr.—Porter Ken
Own.—Kradjian & Porter
1986 2 0 0 0 $1,500
1985 10 2 3 2 $55,125
Lifetime 12 2 3 2 $56,625

12Mar86-8SA 6½f :214 :451 1:172sy 11 114 46 46 54 511 Solis A3 Baldwin 72-25 JettingHome,RoylTresure,ElCorzon 6
29Jan86-8SA 1⅟16 :462 1:11 1:43 ft 50 114 42½ 53 65 79½ Solis A4 Sta Ctlna 77-15 Ferdinand,VrietyRod,GrndAllegince 8
31Dec85-8SA 6f :214 :444 1:103ft 4½ 114 1hd 2hd 2hd 2½ StevensGL1 Sn Miguel 84-15 DancingPirte,SmokeyOrbit,HyKing 3
31Dec85—Bumped off stride start
23Nov85-8Hol 7f :214 :443 1:23 ft 8½ 117 3nk 42 64½ 57¾ PincyLJr4 Hol Prvu 82-13 JudgeSmells,RaisedOnStage,OldBid 8
23Nov85—Grade III; Steadied at 3/8
13Nov85-7Hol 6f :23 :473 1:122gd 2½ 117 1hd 2hd 1½ 12½ McCarronCJ1 Aw22000 77-26 SmokeyOrbit,LyA.C.,RmblingMontl 7
13Nov85—Bumped stretch
23Oct85-7SA 1 :47 1:121 1:393ft 7½ 114 21 2hd 2½ 21½ Hernandez R3 Aw26000 68-25 BdgerLnd,SmokeyOrbit,RisdOnStg 7
20Oct85-8SA 7f :221 :451 1:233ft 3½ 115 64¾ 65¾ 64½ 57 DelhoussyeE3 Sny Slp 75-17 LouisianSlew,SnowChief,DonB.Blue 8
20Oct85—Bumped, jostled at 3 1/2
28Aug85-8Dmr 1 :461 1:111 1:363ft 25 114 54½ 58 59 37 ShomkrW4 Balboa 78-16 Swear, Bright Tom, Smokey Orbit 8
28Aug85—Grade III; Steadied at 7/8
14Aug85-8Dmr 6f :22 :451 1:102ft 13 114 56 57½ 411 36½ Stevens G L1 De Anza 88-13 BolgerMgic,ClerChoice,SmokyOrbit 5
14Aug85—Wide
2Aug85-3Dmr 6f :221 :451 1:101ft 10 116 44½ 35½ 44½ 27 Stevens G L6 Aw10000 80-18 Swear, Smokey Orbit, Fallen Line 6
2Aug85—Wide into stretch
Mar 27 SA ⓣ 3f fm :393 h (d) Mar 22 SA 5f ft :592 h Mar 6 SA ⓣ 5f fm 1:031 h (d) Feb 26 SA 4f ft :474 h

***Delapre** — B. c. 3, by He Loves Me—Northampton, by Northfields
STEVENS G L — 114 — Br.—Newsome T J (Eng) — Tr.—Matthews S G
Own.—Caracciolo-Eigner-Matthews
1986 1 0 0 1 $6,000
1985 8 2 3 1 $8,045
Turf 9 2 3 2 $14,045
Lifetime 9 2 3 2 $14,045

27Feb86-8SA a6½f ⓣ:22 :4521:161fm 9 114 1hd 1½ 1hd 31 Stevens G L8 Aw40000 77-22 RomnMgestrite,MoorgteMn,Delpr 10
10Sep85♦3Pontefract(Eng) 1 1:454gd *4 129 ⓣ 13 CuthenS Thorpe Nrsy H Delpre,FrenchFlutter,DoonVentur 13
28Aug85♦6Wolverhamp'n(Eng 7f 1:321gd *3-2 133 ⓣ 21½ CarsonW Mrvle Nrsy H BakersDough, Delapre, Octiga 7
10Aug85♦2Lingfield(Eng) 7f 1:283sf 5 125 ⓣ 2¾ Hills R Cruise Nrsy H ParkiesBar, Delapre, Stangrave 7
3Aug85♦2Thirsk(Eng) 7f 1:282gd 4½ 126 ⓣ 35 KmbrlyA Brdfrd Nrsy H Handspring, StSepulchre, Delapre 11
10Jly85♦1Brighton(Eng) 7f 1:25 fm 3½ 126 ⓣ 1no StrtR Woodngdn(Mdn) Delapre, North King, Asaaf 10
15Jun85♦7Carlisle(Eng) 6f 1:16 gd *3-2 126 ⓣ 67¼ Hide E Lngtwn(Mdn) Seclusive,LivingShrp,AnglinHome 13
3Jun85♦2Bath(Eng) a5½f 1:111fm 10 123 ⓣ 21½ Hills R Downs EmpireBlue,Delpre,MountDominion 8
20May85♦1Wolverhamp'n(Eng 5f 1:031gd 20 126 ⓣ 611 Hills R Penkridge(Mdn) Shelhoub, Anbaal, Labrag 17
Mar 22 Hol 5f ft 1:012 h Mar 7 Hol 5f ft 1:021 h Feb 23 Hol 5f ft 1:004 h ●Feb 11 Hol 5f ft 1:00 h

***Stratford East** — B. c. 3, by Tyrnavos—Star Face, by African Sky
TORO F — 114 — Br.—Trotter Mrs J (Eng) — Tr.—Velasquez Danny
Own.—Kovnick & Paasch
1986 2 0 0 0
1985 4 1 1 1 $4,351
Turf 4 1 1 1 $4,351
Lifetime 6 1 1 1 $4,351

21Mar86-6SA 6½f :211 :434 1:164ft 80 1105 55 69½ 57 64 HamiltonMA1 Aw20000 82-15 RoylTresure,Beu'sLedr,TripoliShors 9
21Mar86—Pinched at start
2Mar86-6SA 1⅟16 :454 1:104 1:43 ft 90 114 1113 1111 1014 1018¼ Meza R Q1 Aw30000 67-13 ImpriousSpirt,IcyGroom,Scrpbook 11
2Mar86—Broke slowly
19Sep85♦3Yarmouth(Eng) 1 1:373gd 12 128 ⓣ 712 CuthnS Albrt Bton Nrsy H Open Hero, Hills Bid, Sohail 9
27Jun85♦3Salisbury(Eng) 6f 1:181gd 5 128 ⓣ 38 CthnS Veuv Clcqt Chmpgn Chalk Stream, Lance,StratfordEast 4
17Jun85♦1Nottingham(Eng) 5f 1:024gd *7-5 126 ⓣ 1hd EddryP Blckbstrs(Mdn) StrtfordEst,CJmBlus,MmmysScrt 12
10Jun85♦1Leicester(Eng) 5f 1:034gd 2 126 ⓣ 21½ Day N Wolvey(Mdn) Bold Spy, Stratford East, Vitsari 11
Mar 19 SA 4f gd :481 hg Mar 13 SA 6f m 1:144 h Feb 26 SA 1 ft 1:424 h ●Feb 21 SA 7f sl 1:312 h

***Moorgate Man** — Ch. c. 3, by Remainder Man—Silly Woman, by Silly Season
MCCARRON C J — 121 — Br.—Dedford Stud (Eng) — Tr.—Mitchell Mike
Own.—Bavasi-Kerlan-Lndn et al
1986 1 0 1 0 $8,000
1985 8 4 1 1 $43,532
Turf 8 4 2 1 $51,532
Lifetime 9 4 2 1 $51,532

27Feb86-8SA a6½f ⓣ:22 :4521:161fm *2½ 121 52½ 62½ 2hd 21 McCarronCJ3 Aw40000 77-22 RomnMgestrite,MoorgteMn,Delpr 10
27Feb86—Bumped at 1/16; floated out final 1/16
29Nov85-8Hol 1 :451 1:11 1:37 sy 4 116 23 615 626 — McCrrnCJ2 Hst Th Flg — — DarbyFair,SnowChief,AcksLikRuler 6
29Nov85—Pulled up
22Sep85♦4Longchamp(Fra) a7f 1:22 gd 4½ 123 ⓣ 62¼ SbrWR Px dl Slmndr(Gr1) BiserVole,ReglStle,BoldArrngmnt 10
13Aug85♦4Newcastle(Eng) 7f 1:302gd 4½ 126 ⓣ 12 Eddery P Stn Dlvl(Gr3) MoorgtMn,BoldArrngmnt,Rckstrw 10
20Jun85♦5Ascot(Eng) 6f 1:151gd 4½ 123 ⓣ 38 Piggott L Chesham Bakharoff, Akaeleel, MoorgateMan 8
18Jun85♦4Ascot(Eng) 6f 1:144gd 7½ 123 ⓣ 21½ EdderyP Coventry(Gr3) SureBlade,MoorgateMan,Cliveden 12
1May85♦5Ascot(Eng) 5f 1:023gd 4 127 ⓣ 1no Miller M Garter MoorgateMan,Nomintion,Shelhoub 6
22Apr85♦1Windsor(Eng) 5f 1:022gd *1-2 128 ⓣ 13 Miller M Trllgr Sqr MoorgateMan,DeltaLima,WyAbove 6
12Apr85♦1Kempton(Eng) 5f 1:094sf *3-2 126 ⓣ 15 EdderyP Plynths(Mdn) MoorgateMan, Hotbee, Teetoy 8
●Mar 15 Hol 3f gd :352 h Mar 9 Hol 4f ft :483 h Feb 22 Hol 6f ft 1:151 hg Feb 17 Hol 5f sy 1:00 h

Halo's Sword — Ch. c. 3, by Halo—Sword Ballet, by Damascus
MCHARGUE D G — 114 — Br.—David's Farm (Ky) — Tr.—Sullivan John — 1986 — Turf
Own.—Brillembourg J D — Lifetime 5 1 2 0 $2,743
19Oct85 4Naas(Ire) 6f 1:151gd 5½ 114 ① 1213 GlspD RdSastBrdthrNrsyH TheBeanDk
28Sep85 2DownRoyal(Ire) 7f :sf 2 129 ① 21½ Roche C Strmvle Plt FlashOfStee
28Sep85—No time taken
19Sep85 5Thurles(Ire) 1 1:413gd *2-3 126 ① 11½ GilespiD LschI Plt(Mdn) Hlo'sSword
31Aug85 4Curragh(Ire) a6½f 1:191sf 6 122 ① 44 GillespiD Anglsy(Gr3) Woodman,Rc
24Aug85 7PhoenixPk(Ire) 7f 1:273sf 20 126 ① 21 GilspD RhnGrpPlt(Mdn) Cabinteely,
Mar 24 SA ① 5f fm 1:023 h (d) Mar 19 SA 4f gd :501 h Mar 4 SA 6f ft 1:15 h Feb 27 SA

Bold And Greene — B. c. 3, by Shecky Greene—Bold Coquetta, by Bold
PINCAY L JR — 114 — Br.—Monumental Farms Inc (Ky) — Tr.—Winick Randy — 1986 — 1985
Own.—Monumental Farms Inc — Lifetime 6 1 0 1 $22,300
9Mar86-1SA 1 :451 1:103 1:381sy 4 117 34 49½ 514 518¾ Stevens G L3 Aw31000 58-19 Lightnin
9Mar86—Bobbled start
26Feb86-8SA 6f :213 :441 1:09 ft 15 118 43 42½ 53 35¾ DlhssE10 Bolsa Chica 87-16 Ketoh, Z
26Feb86—Wide into stretch
7Feb86-1SA 6½f :212 :434 1:153ft 2½ 120 33 32 33½ 52½ DelhoussyeE7 Aw26000 88-12 B.A.Adjs
12Jan86-3SA 6f :211 :434 1:09 ft 3½ 118 1hd 11½ 14 16½ Pincay L Jr1 Mdn 93-11 BoldAnd
26Dec85-4SA 6f :212 :442 1:102ft 5 117 2½ 21 22½ 44¼ Valenzuela P A10 Mdn 82-13 Atom'sT
1Dec85-6Hol 6f :222 :462 1:122gd 2½ 118 41½ 43 44½ 64¾ Delahoussaye E6 Mdn 77-16 Jewelry
1Dec85—Bumped at start
Mar 26 SA 4f ft :47 h ●Mar 7 SA 4f ft :462 h Feb 22 SA 5f ft :591 h ●Feb 16 SA

Prince Bobby B. — B. c. 3, by King Pellinore—Riviere Bleue, by Riverman
OLIVARES F — 114 — Br.—Lerner P (Ky) — Tr.—Bernstein David — 1986 — 1985
Own.—Bernstein D — Lifetime 4 1 0 0 $15,250
9Mar86-1SA 1 :451 1:103 1:381sy *9-5 117 1hd 2hd 38½ 410½ McCarronCJ2 Aw31000 67-19 Lightnin
8Feb86-8SA 7f :222 :444 1:231ft 2½ 114 1½ 1hd 21½ 54½ McCrrCJ7 Sn Vcnte 88-19 GrndAlle
8Feb86—Grade III; Bumped start
26Jan86-4SA 6½f :214 :441 1:15 ft *9-5 118 1½ 12½ 17 18 McCarron C J3 Mdn 95-12 PrncBob
6Oct85-6SA 6f :214 :451 1:101ft 8½ 117 2½ 31½ 36½ 513 McHargue D G5 Mdn 74-16 JudgeSm
●Mar 23 SA 6f ft 1:113 h ●Mar 2 SA 1 ft 1:38 h Feb 24 SA 7f ft 1:262 h Feb 18 SA

In Toto — B. c. 3, by Mr Prospector—Solartic, by Briartic
SIBILLE R — 114 — Br.—Juddmonte Farms (Ky) — Tr.—Gosden John H M — 1986
Own.—Juddmonte Farms — Lifetime 3 1 1 0 $4,601 — Turf
31Jly85 3Goodwood(Eng) 6f 1:133gd 4 123 ① 89¾ EdderyP Richmond(Gr2) Nomination
31Jly85—Dead heat
1Jun85 1Kempton(Eng) 5f :591gd *1-3 126 ① 14 CthnS Rivermead(Mdn) In Toto, Kin
17May85 6Newbury(Eng) 5f 1:031gd 2½ 123 ① 2no Eddery P May Fayruz, In T
Mar 25 Hol 5f ft 1:02 h Mar 15 Hol 5f gd 1:01 h ●Mar 8 Hol 6f ft 1:12 h Mar 3 Hol

Tommy The Hawk — Ch. c. 3, by Judgable—Boiled in Oil, by Donut King
DELAHOUSSAYE E — 114 — Br.—Putnam G (Cal) — Tr.—Mulhall Richard W — 1986 — 1985
Own.—Putnam G — Lifetime 13 1 3 2 $36,485
26Mar86-6SA 1⅛ :454 1:104 1:43 ft 28 114 310 87½ 89½ 713½ Hawley S5 Aw30000 73-13 Imperious
14Feb86-8SA 1 :454 1:11 1:363ft 9 115 64½ 51½ 41½ 62¾ Kaenel J L7 Aw28000 82-16 Big Play,
29Jan86-8SA 1⅛ :462 1:11 1:43 ft 74 116 32 32½ 54 56½ DlhossyE5 Sta Ctlna 80-15 Ferdinand
29Jan86—Wide into stretch
4Jan86-8SA 1 :453 1:103 1:361ft 13 114 1hd 1hd 32 47½ Meza R Q4 Ls Feliz 88-13 Badger L
1Jan86-6SA 6f :214 :44 1:082ft 8½ 118 54½ 57½ 79½ 710¾ DlhoussyE7 Aw24000 85-13 GrndAlly
1Jan86—Wide into stretch
22Dec85-7Hol 7f :223 :453 1:231ft 17 115 51½ 41 43 44½ Meza RQ2 Rvng Boy 84-17 HyKing
22Dec85—Bumped start
7Dec85-4Hol 6f :22 :45 1:103ft 4 119 87½ 64¾ 54 33¾ DelhoussyeE8 Aw20000 87-12 Mjestic
11Nov85-6SA 1 :464 1:123 1:40 gd 3½ 117 2½ 2½ 2hd 1no DelahoussyeE5 Mdn 68-26 TommyTh
11Nov85—Bumped into stretch
30Oct85-6SA 6f :214 :45 1:10 ft 4 117 73½ 53 22 24 DelahoussyeE9 Mdn 84-14 TimToSm
30Oct85—Lugged in stretch
19Oct85-6SA 6½f :214 :451 1:174ft 13 117 42 41½ 33½ 32 McHargueDG10 Mdn 79-13 FrstStrm
19Oct85—Broke slowly; lugged in stretch
Mar 26 SA 6f ft 1:14 h Mar 20 SA 6f ft 1:141 h Feb 24 SA 5f ft :59 h Feb 6 SA 4f

El Corazon — B. c. 3, by Raja Baba—Bar's Dream, by Your Host
LIPHAM T — 114 — Br.—Jones Jr & Farish III (Ky) — Tr.—Fanning Jerry — 1986 — 1985
Own.—Singer C B — Lifetime 8 0 4 1 $24,865
12Mar86-8SA 6½f :214 :451 1:172sy 17 114 32½ 32½ 3½ 37 Lipham T5 Baldwin 76-25 JettingHo
1Mar86-6SA 6f :214 :45 1:101ft 11 118 52½ 3½ 11 2½ Lipham T7 Mdn 86-16 BabySlew
26Jan86-4SA 6½f :214 :441 1:15 ft 7½ 118 32 44½ 613 1122½ Toro F8 Mdn 72-12 PrncBobb

Following are the horses' best class ratings, along with the dates of each. The notation S4-27 means a sprint having a competitive quality rating of 4 in which a horse earned 27 class points. That's the top rating for Smokey Orbit, the inside post horse in this field.

Horses	Class Ratings	Dates
Smokey Orbit	S4–27	Dec. 31
Delapre	S3–26	Feb. 27
Stratford East	S3–21	Mar. 21
Moorgate Man	S3–26	Feb. 27
Halo's Sword	No rating	x
Bold And Greene	R4–12	Mar. 9
	S4–37	Feb. 26
	S4–24	Jan. 12
Prince Bobby B.	S4–45	Feb. 8
	S3–21	Jan. 26
Tommy The Hawk	R4–22	Feb. 14
	R4–43	Jan. 29
	R4–23	Jan. 4
B.A. Adjustment	S3–28	Mar. 12
	S3–34	Feb. 26
	S1–7	Feb. 1
Passer II	No rating	x

Which three-year-old is the class of the field? One horse actually qualifies, but on class ratings alone three possibilities jump out: Prince Bobby B. (45) earned the top rating in the field against the most advanced competition, a Grade 3 stakes; Tommy The Hawk (43) earned its high figure routing in the restricted Santa Catalina stakes won by Ferdinand over the impressive Variety Road; Bold And Greene (37) did its best so far in the restricted sprint stakes won by the tragic Ketoh over rugged Zabaleta.

Also meriting consideration is Moorgate Man (26), twice-raced in the states but a Group 3 winner and consistent solid stakes performer at two in England and France. Second following a troubled trip when favored on this course Feb. 27, Moorgate Man retains the services of champion Chris McCarron and has the credentials to improve.

At this point handicappers have developed a strong sense of the class hierarchy in the field, but a capitulation to full-dress handicapping embracing all the available information surpasses hasty decision making when still-developing nonclaiming three-year-olds are featured. The objective is to unearth information that either supports or weakens the case for the individuals having the highest ratings.

The conditions of the Charles Whittingham conspire to expose immature horses to an unusual distance on grass footing against stakes-caliber competition. It takes a fancy three-year-old to win. Moreover, in southern California better threes regularly falter when first they try turf, as the speed-conscious efforts on the main track do not transport readily to the softer lawn. It's reassuring to know a three-year-old has been bred to like grass, and can be rated besides.

Moorgate Man was favored at even money, which eliminates the import summarily. I trust handicappers understand that. With its main opposition sporting a class rating almost twice as great, an even-money shot would have to improve tremendously to warrant any further consideration. Let's assume Moorgate Man has been overbet in relation to real chances, which it has.

Tommy The Hawk has disappointed twice since collecting its big rating against Ferdinand and company January 29. It should have shown to better advantage in nonwinners allowance company. Perhaps the January race's main competition deserved a class rating Tommy The Hawk did not? No play.

Bold And Greene broke its maiden when favored by a strong positive rail bias January 12, is the front-running type that will not secure the lead today, and is not bred for turf. No additional information bolsters a class rating on dirt that is third-best here.

B.A. Adjustment (34) lacks grass parents, too, and has been overrated since its maiden score at 13 to 1 February 7. That day also featured an extra strong rail bias, as did many the first half of Santa Anita 1986. Notice the maiden win ratings earned by B.A. Adjustment and Prince Bobby B., respectively. Each horse won big in fast style, but B.A. Adjustment earned 7 points and Prince Bobby B. 21. The difference is that B.A. Adjustment won straight while Prince Bobby B. had lots of energy left. The latter horse received a projected rating. The difference is obviously crucial.

Now look in-depth at the high-rated colt, Prince Bobby B., which is always advisable policy. The King Pellinore colt stands out. Its high rating is bolstered by blue-blooded grass breeding top and bottom and by sizzling best-of-morning workouts at distances both longer and shorter than today's. Prince Bobby B. might have tested graded stakes conditions prematurely, as many ill-managed three-year-olds do, but it deported itself nicely at that level and should be too much thoroughbred for the restricted brand of stakes horses it meets today.

The result chart on page 131 shows just how superior Prince Bobby B. proved to be. Chalk up a nice score for numerical class ratings and full-blown handicapping in tandem. The mutuel is juicy, an overlay.

Record Keeping. To use the method well, handicappers need par times for each track on the circuit, daily track variants, adjusted times, the class-speed charts on pages 70 and 72, the CQ Scale ratings of races, and a record of the basic class ratings earned by the winners of each race. To obtain the CQ Scale ratings, they also need an opportunity to observe the races.

EIGHTH RACE
Santa Anita
MARCH 28, 1986

ABOUT 6 ½ FURLONGS.(Turf). (1.11⅘) 2nd Running of THE CHARLES WHITTINGHAM STAKES. $42,000 added. 3-year-olds which are non-winners of a sweepstakes since December 25. (Allowance) Weight, 121 lbs. Non-winners of a race of $20,000 any time allowed 3 lbs.; of $15,000 since December 25, 5 lbs.; of such a race since October 1 or $13,000 since December 25, 7 lbs. Closed 11:00 a.m. Tuesday, March 25 at $50 each with 16 nominations. (Claiming races not considered.)

Value of race $42,800; value to winner $23,900; second $8,400; third $6,300; fourth $3,150; fifth $1,050. Mutuel pool $490,525.

Last Raced	Horse	Eqt.	A.	Wt	PP	St	¼	½	Str	Fin	Jockey	Odds $1
9Mar86 ^{1}SA^4	Prince Bobby B.	b	3	114	7	3	3½	1^1	1^5	1^8	Olivares F	5.50
2Mar86 ^{6}SA^7	Tommy The Hawk	b	3	116	8	8	$9^{1½}$	9^{hd}	7^1	2^{hd}	Delahoussaye E	36.30
27Feb86 ^{8}SA^3	Delapre		3	114	2	6	5^1	5½	3^{hd}	3½	Stevens G L	4.80
12Mar86 ^{8}SA^6	B. A. Adjustment		3	116	9	2	1½	2^{hd}	$2^{1½}$	$4^{1½}$	Solis A	23.60
21Mar86 ^{6}SA^6	Stratford East	b	3	115	3	9	8½	$8^{1½}$	6^{hd}	5^{hd}	Toro F	28.60
27Feb86 ^{8}SA^2	Moorgate Man		3	121	4	7	7^5	$6^{1½}$	5^2	6¾	McCarron C J	1.00
12Mar86 ^{8}SA^5	Smokey Orbit	b	3	116	1	5	4½	$3^{1½}$	4^{hd}	7½	Kaenel J L	56.00
19Oct85 ^{4}Ire^{12}	Halo's Sword		3	116	5	10	10	10	$8^{3½}$	$8^{5½}$	McHargue D G	44.30
1Dec85 ^{7}Mex^1	Passer II		3	121	10	1	2^{hd}	4^{hd}	9½	9^{nk}	Valenzuela P A	6.40
9Mar86 ^{1}SA^5	Bold And Greene		3	117	6	4	6½	7^1	10	10	Pincay L Jr	9.70

OFF AT 4:50. Start good. Won easily. Time, :21⅘, :44⅘, 1:08⅘, 1:15⅕ Course firm.

$2 Mutuel Prices:				
	7-PRINCE BOBBY B.	13.00	6.60	4.40
	8-TOMMY THE HAWK		25.60	9.60
	2-DELAPRE			3.40

B. c, by King Pellinore—Riviere Bleue, by Riverman. Trainer Bernstein David. Bred by Lerner P (Ky).

PRINCE BOBBY B. always prominent, took over while under a snug hold after a quarter, then drew off in the stretch to win as much the best. TOMMY THE HAWK, devoid of early foot, was forced to lose ground when quite wide into the stretch, lugged inward to bump BOLD AND GREENE near the furlong marker, continued to lug in despite left-handed pressure and was up for the place while never a threat to the winner. DELAPRE, in contention early, lacked the needed response in the drive. B. A. ADJUSTMENT led early, yielded the advantage to PRINCE BOBBY B. after a quarter, continued forwardly to the final furlong, then gave way. STRATFORD EAST, outrun early, bobbled soon after the start and was never prominent. MOORGATE MAN, in a contending position early, began faltering after a half and bobbled soon after crossing the main track. SMOKEY ORBIT, a bit slow to begin, moved up quickly to attend the pace for a half, then also faltered. HALO'S SWORD was forced to steady when lacking room. PASSER II near the pace for a half, also was forced to steady when lacking racing room in midstretch. BOLD AND GREENE checked when in close quarters not too long after the start, was bumped off stride by TOMMY THE HAWK near the furlong marker and gave way badly.

Owners— 1, Bernstein D; 2, Putnam G; 3, Caracciolo-Eigner-Matthews; 4, Santa Barbara Stb (Lessee); 5, Kovnick & Paasch; 6, Bavasi-Kerlan-Lndn et al; 7, Kradjian & Porter; 8, Brillembourg J D; 9, Buck-Cain-Rionda; 10, Monumental Farms Inc.

Trainers— 1, Bernstein David; 2, Mulhall Richard W; 3, Matthews S G; 4, Vienna Darrell; 5, Velasquez Danny; 6, Mitchell Mike; 7, Porter Ken; 8, Sullivan John; 9, Barrera Lazaro S; 10, Winick Randy.

Overweight: Tommy The Hawk 2 pounds; Stratford East 1; Smokey Orbit 2; Halo's Sword 2; Bold And Greene

Class ratings can be kept economically in a notebook, if not a computerized file or data base. Look at Table 11.

The data are extracted from my notes for April 4 at Santa Anita 1986. The calculations for a nine-race program consume roughly twenty minutes, and these include race shapes besides class ratings.

Along the top row the numerals beside the letter notations S and R are the daily track variants. On April 4 Santa Anita was Slow 1 to the half in sprints, Slow 2 at the wire. For routes, the track surface played Slow 3, Slow 3.

The data below the column numerals can be read as follows:

1. The conditions of eligibility. The C40 means the first race was written for $40,000 claiming horses.

2. In parentheses are the individual race variants in relation to par at the fractional call and final call.
3. The distance of the race is expressed as S (sprint) or R
   (route).
4. Adjusted times, fractional and final, after daily variants have been added or subtracted.
5. Race shapes, or configurations of pace, such as F-F,
   meaning the first race was fast early and fast late in relation to par.
6. CQ Scale ratings and the basic class ratings earned by
   the winners.

Examining Table 11, which winner ran the best race of the
day? It's the winner of the featured 8th, whose 48 class rating is
18 points or 60 percent greater than the class par of 30 for classified allowance races.

Which winner ran the next best race April 4? It's the pair of
maiden-claiming graduates, as each resisted Strongly Competitive challenges and earned a class rating of 14, which is 40 percent above the class par of 10 (half the class par for open
$32,000 claiming races).

TABLE 11 Class Ratings and Related Notebook Data for April 4, 1986, at Santa Anita Park						
April 4 ①	②	③	S −1 −2	R ④	−3 −3 ⑤	Class ⑥
1. c40 (−1 +2)		R	111^3	138	F – F	3–27
2. c10 (−3 −5)		S	45^3	111^3	S – S	4–4
3. MdCl (−2 −3) $32		S	45^3	111^3	A – A	4–14
4. MdCl (−1 −2) $32		S	45^2	111^2	A – A	4–14
5. NWMC(turf route)						
6. MdCl (−3 −7) $50		R	111^3	139^4	A – S	2–6
7. c25 (+2 0)		S	44^2	116^1	F – F	3–18
8. Clf (−1 +2)		Ⓣ S	44^3	114^4	A – F	4–48
9. cl2,5(−5 −3)		R	112	144^4	A – A	3–9

Which race is next best?

It's the first, whose winner finished 6 class points or 28 percent faster than par of 21. The winner of the 7th race also exceeded par (15), by 20 percent.

How much below the class pars have the winners of the second and 6th races been rated?

The second-race winner is 33 percent below par of 6, and the winner of the 6th finished 50 percent below par of 12.

By similar critique handicappers can quickly review the daily programs.

Experience with the numbers crystallizes the relationships among the various horses within each class as well as between levels. The final chapter presents two statistical techniques for accomplishing that, and much much more.

Computer Storage. Any spreadsheet application or data base software for personal computers can store these data with remarkable flexibility and ease. The matrix of Table 12 shows a computer format that can retrieve instantaneously the year's class ratings for every horse on the grounds.

The top rows contain the conditions of eligibility in notational form and the class pars-top ratings at each level.

Selected horses by age and sex fill the left-hand columns. Their class ratings for the season fill the columns under the appropriate competitive headings. Sprints and routes are identified by letters, and the asterisk means a winning race. Race dates have not been entered, but might. In the lower half of a spreadsheet application the same matrix would be repeated for claiming horses. Many horses, such as Bedouin in the table, will appear in both divisions.

By scanning the terminal screen any horse's full array of class ratings for the year by class level are readily retrieved, sorted, and evaluated. Rows can be moved and juxtaposed, meaning a specific field of horses can be examined conveniently in past-performance format.

From these few data, considerable insight can be inferred. Look at the three-year-olds Royal Treasure and Zabaleta. Assume the race dates are chronological left to right and up and

TABLE 12
Selected Class Ratings by Competitive Levels for Nonclaiming and Claiming Horses in Computerized Spreadsheet Format

Conditions of Eligibility with Class Pars and Top Ratings

Nonclaiming Horses

Horses (Age/Sex)	Mdn 15–35	Alw NW1x 21–45	Alw NW2x 24–50	Alw NW3x4x 27–60	Clf Alw 30–65	Stk R-0 36–80	Stk L-Gr 3 42–90	Stk Gr 2-Gr 1 48–100
Bedouin (5 H)								
Five North (5 H)		S24 S18 S20		R22 R22	S10	S60 S34		
Royal Treasure (3 C)	S0 S18*	S8				S47		
Zabaleta (3 C)	S30*					S41		S54*

Claiming Horses

Claiming Horses	$10,000 & Below 6–20	$12,500–16,000 9–25	$20,000–25,000 15–35	$32,000–40,000 21–45	$50,000–62,500 24–50	Above $62,500 30–65
Bedouin (5 H)	R4*	R13	R16* R10	R28* R36*	R32*	
Growler Sandue (4 C)			S17 S19	S4 S24 S20 S28		
Green Coleen (4 F)		S8 S9*	S21* S10			

* Winning race

down, which is normally true of three-year-olds passing through basic conditions.

Which is the better horse?

It's clearly Zabaleta.

Zabaleta's record reveals it won its maiden first out while earning twice as many points as the class par. It skipped the routine nonwinners races and next performed better-than-par in two stakes efforts. In its third try Zabaleta won a Grade 2 sprint, no less, the Bay Shore at seven furlongs in New York.

Royal Treasure is no slouch either. After getting no points in its debut, it rebounded to conquer maidens in a performance better-than-par. Already Royal Treasure has performed well above-par in an open stakes, earning 47 points. This colt should have little difficulty returning to preliminary nonwinners allowance conditions, where the highest rating is 50, and winning twice.

What is Bedouin's best class level?

The five-year-old notched five races during the Santa Anita season, all claimers, but it looked sharpest against $40,000 horses. It beat $50,000 horses while getting a slightly lower class rating. Just as clearly, at its best Bedouin is no allowance horse. It needs claiming competition.

Growler Sandue probably wants $25,000 competition to show its best and Green Coleen acts like a $16,000 horse.

Class handicappers with personal computers will rejoice at having fingertip access to numbers that reflect demonstrated abilities against specific opposition. The record keeping is child's play. Horses' names, age, and sex are entered once. Class ratings can be updated weekly.

Whether modern handicappers resort to personal computers or manual files to store the numbers, the new class-rating method advances the cause of class handicapping everywhere. Armed now with numbers, practitioners can spot the best horses at a glance.

To anyone willing to make a deeper commitment to class handicapping as the systematic method of choice, the next chapter paves the way to a higher order of financial success.

9

Blueboys

Identifying the best horses of succeeding generations consti-
tutes one of the most gratifying amusements of thoroughbred
handicapping. That is the province of class handicappers, but a
responsibility not very effectively discharged in that chamber
until now.

This chapter supplies two elementary statistical tools that
will separate the wheat from the chaff of each new thoroughbred crop. The objective is to distinguish the potential champs
and division leaders from the others. In knowledgeable, practiced hands, the tools transport even recreational practitioners
beyond mere entertainment and toward profits.

The relative quality of any performance at any competitive
level can be estimated by comparing a horse's class rating to
the class par. The ratio of the numbers expresses the strength
of an individual performance in relation to winners, runners-
up, and close finishers as a group. The ratio yields a performance index which can be used to predict the class ratings
horses might be expected to earn at closely related levels, on
the rise, thereby permitting convenient comparisons among
step-ups and horses already tested at the higher level. Several
ratios considered jointly can be accepted as a performance

index which compares unfamiliar horses more reliably, including shippers.

The calculation is elementary:

$$\text{Performance Index (PI)} = \frac{\text{Class Rating}}{\text{Class Par}}$$

The resulting index will range from 0.00 to 2.00, or slightly above 2.00.

An index of 1.00 represents a typical or par performance for the class.

An index of 2.00 means twice as strong a performance as is typical at the class, and an index of 0.50 means half as strong as typical.

Indexes of 1.50 or greater can be accepted as indicating relatively high class at the level and impending success at closely related classes.

For developing horses moving through basic nonwinners allowance conditions and into restricted and lower-level open stakes, the performance index can be trusted to estimate the class ratings that might be earned today. Handicappers multiply today's class par by a horse's PI.

If today's race brings together three-year-olds and up that have never won two races other than maiden or claiming, the class par is 24. A three-year-old earning a PI of 1.33 for its maiden and first nonwinners allowance win would be expected to achieve a 32 rating today.

How well does that compare to horses that have already competed impressively at today's level?

To arrive at reliable performance indexes for older horses, handicappers should remember that recent consistency outperforms consistency. Probability studies have indicated that recent consistency refers to the previous six races. Identify the latest half-dozen races that have been representative and select the three highest PIs. Sum the three and divide by three. The resulting index qualifies as a measure of ability and stability in combination.

For developing horses, lightly raced threes and twos, and younger four-year-olds of winter as well, handicappers instead focus on the "good" performances in the existing record.

"Good" performances have been defined as wins or in-the-money finishes within two lengths in sprints, within three lengths in routes. At times close finishes can supplant in-the-money finishes, as handicappers decide. Discount the awful or inexplicable efforts that creep into the records of younger horses. The poor races are a routine component of the competitive seasoning process and are not representative.

Examine Table 13. It shows the performance indexes for the entire season of the seven horses that competed in the 1986 Santa Anita Derby. What can handicappers infer from the table that the crowd might overlook?

We begin with a blazer.

In two starts at Santa Anita the popular pre–Kentucky Derby favorite Snow Chief could not approach a PI of 1.00. Its combined PI is 0.74, meaning it should obtain approximately three-quarters the class points allocated to par (48) in Grade 1 events. Snow Chief earned exactly that number of class points in the Santa Anita Derby, a race it plundered by six lengths. In the aftermath, Snow Chief's Santa Anita Derby score was widely overrated. Class handicappers applying Blueboy ratings would have backed away from the colt after comparing its PI with those of other starters at Churchill Downs, certainly at the stingy odds (2 to 1)

Icy Groom's three best PIs combine for an index of 1.09, but the colt has not approached that number in Grade 1 competition. By comparing the combined index with the PI achieved under specific conditions of eligibility, handicappers sense whether a certain class level has been significantly more or less troublesome. The inspection assists in classifying horses more accurately. By this technique, Icy Groom looks a cut or two below Grade 1 so far.

Ferdinand illustrates a few more interesting guideposts. First, its Santa Anita Derby performance (PI = 0.65) should be discarded. The track surface was "greasy," as trainer Charles Whittingham termed it, from overnight rains, and Ferdinand cannot conduct himself confidently on slick surfaces. The son of Nijinski II ran an unrepresentative race, and unrepresentative performances do not count. Off-tracks, troubled trips, biased paths, poor jockeying, preps for conditioning pur-

TABLE 13

Performance Indexes (PIs) for the
1986 Santa Anita Derby Horses

Horses	Dates	Competitive Levels	Class Pars	Class Ratings	PIs	Combined PI
Snow Chief	Apr 6	Gr 1	48	36 (1^6)	0.75	0.74
	Mar 1	Gr 1	48	-not available-		
	Feb 2	Gr 3	42	-not available-		
	Jan 12	Stk-R	36	30 (1)	0.83	
Icy Groom	Apr 6	Gr 1	48	31 (2^6)	0.65	1.09
	Mar 19	Stk-R	36	36 (1)	1.00	
	Mar 2	NWMC	21	27 (2^1)	1.28	
	Feb 1	Mdn	15	15 (1)	1.00	
	Jan 19	Mdn	15	0	0.00	
Ferdinand	Apr 6	Gr 1	48	31 (3^7)	0.65	1.15
	Mar 22	Gr 2	48	64 ($2^{1/4}$)	1.33	
	Jan 29	Stk-R	36	48 (1)	1.33	
	Jan 4	Stk-R	36	28 (2^{hd})	0.78	
Big Play	Apr 6	Gr 1	48	31 (4^8)	0.65	1.09
	Mar 16	Gr 1	48	43 (2^6)	0.90	
	Feb 14	NWMC	21	24 (1)	1.14	
	Jan 29	Stk-R	36	44 (4^6)	1.22	
	Jan 20	Mdn Clm	10	14 (1)	1.40	
Imperious Spirit	Apr 6	Gr 1	48	28 (5^9)	0.58	1.26
	Mar 19	Stk-R	36	34 (2^2)	0.94	
	Mar 2	NWMC	21	28 (1)	1.33	
	Feb 2	NWMC	21	31 (3^2)	1.50	
	Jan 19	NWMC	21	14 (6^3)	0.67	
Variety Road	Apr 6	Gr 1	48	28 (5^9)	0.58	1.33
	Mar 16	Gr 1	48	48 (1)	1.00	
	Feb 22	Gr 2	48	64 (1)	1.33	
	Jan 29	Stk-R	36	48 ($2^{1/2}$)	1.33	
	Jan 12	Stk-R	36	27 (2^4)	0.75	
	Dec 29	Mdn	15	25 (1)	1.67	
Jetting Home	Apr 6	Gr 1	48	28 (7)	0.58	1.10
	Mar 12	Stk-0	36	36 (1)	1.00	
	Feb 22	Gr 2	48	43 (3^7)	0.90	
	Feb 2	NWMC	21	21 (1)	1.00	
	Jan 9	NWMC	21	27 (5^6)	1.28	
	Dec 27	NWMC	21	23 (2^1)	1.10	

NOTE. Finish and beaten-lengths appear in parentheses.

poses—all qualify as unrepresentative races. Do not count them as legitimate, as this merely distorts the ratings. When doubtful, however, handicappers should count a race as representative and not excuse it. Watching the races closely becomes an imperative.

Moreover, to complicate matters wisely, if lightly raced younger horses have demonstrated sudden dramatic improvement, notably if blue-blooded breeding underscores tremendous future potential, handicappers can use the resulting PI as the likeliest best estimate. This is particularly true if the dramatic improvement occurred in a stakes.

On January 29, in a restricted stakes, the same conditions it confronted January 4, Ferdinand earned a significantly improved PI of 1.33, up from a below-par index of 0.78. Next Ferdinand entered a Grade 2 stakes. Its latest PI of 1.33 multiplied by the Grade 2 class par (48) suggested Ferdinand might collect 64 class points while up in class. Ferdinand earned exactly 64 class points March 22, flattering the method, and again obtained a PI of 1.33.

Ferdinand's combined index consisting of its three top ratings would be 1.15, but class handicappers would have every right to accept 1.33 as more representative of a rapidly improving young colt.

Big Play and Imperious Spirit have earned PIs of 1.09 and 1.26 respectively. In calculating Big Play's figure, discard the maiden-claiming index of 1.40, which is more misleading than enlightening. All maiden-claiming indexes are best ignored.

Of Imperious Spirit, its two best PIs were earned when facing nonwinners other than maiden or claiming, but this is just as often fair procedure when evaluating horses below graded and listed stakes competition, as numerous nonwinners allowance races can be rugged enough to transfer well to restricted and open stakes.

In contrast to their combined PIs, the indexes earned by Big Play and Imperious Spirit in the Santa Anita Derby suggest neither horse is Grade 1 material. If the two were entered in another Grade 1 event, handicappers would be mistaken to estimate the horses' class ratings by invoking the combined PIs. Common sense prevails in these situations. Thought dominates procedure. Technique bolsters analysis but does not substitute for it. The two pretenders are simply eliminated as outclassed.

Variety Road has a combined PI of 1.33, tops in the field. Notice its Grade 1 index falls far below what it had earned versus similar on March 16 and February 22. The discrepancy is sometimes explained by physical ailments or by mysterious variations in the form cycle. Variety Road might need a rest or it might have injured itself. In fact, the second possibility had occurred, and Variety Road was put away for months by trainer Bruce Headley. Ignore the unsubstantial rating, obviously.

Jetting Home gets a PI of 1.10, meaning it performs slightly above par in the usual case, similar to Icy Groom and Big Play.

Blueboys. The procedure for distinguishing the best of the best depends upon the proportion of class points a horse can earn at each competitive level as it advances in the division. Now the ratio of class ratings to top ratings signifies the difference.

Examine Table 14.

For the same Santa Anita Derby field, the table describes the percentages of allotted points each horse accumulated in each race of the season.

Icy Groom, for example, achieved 31 percent of the class points available at the Grade 1 level April 6, 45 percent in its restricted stakes win March 19, and 60 percent of the points allocated to nonwinners other than maiden or claiming in its runner-up effort of March 2. In its maiden win, Icy Groom rated a par 15, or 37 percent of the 35 class points allocated to maiden competition.

Blueboy ranks are determined by averaging a pair of the percentage scores:

1. The most recent representative race
2. The best rating against the most advanced competition

The most recent representative race refers to the latest race, provided the performance was not marred by the trip, track bias, track condition, body language, or horse's physical condition. In Table 14 the Santa Anita Derby was disregarded for Ferdinand (track condition) and Variety Road (physical condition), improving the horses' rankings significantly.

TABLE 14
Blueboy Ranks for the 1986
Santa Anita Derby Horses

Horses	Dates	Competitive Levels	Highest Ratings	Class Ratings	Blueboy Ratings	Ranks
Snow Chief	Apr 6	Gr 1	100	36	.36	37*
	Mar 1	Gr 1	100	-not available-		
	Feb 2	Gr 3	90	-not available-		
	Jan 12	Stk-R	80	30	.37	
Icy Groom	Apr 6	Gr 1	100	31	.31	45
	Mar 19	Stk-R	80	36	.45	
	Mar 2	NWMC	45	27	.60	
	Feb 1	Mdn	35	15	.37	
	Jan 19	Mdn	35	0	.00	
Ferdinand	Apr 6	Gr 1	100	31	.31	62
	Mar 22	Gr 2	100	64	.64	
	Jan 29	Stk-R	80	48	.60	
	Jan 4	Stk-R	80	28	.35	
Big Play	Apr 6	Gr 1	100	31	.31	37
	Mar 16	Gr 1	100	43	.43	
	Feb 14	NWMC	45	24	.53	
	Jan 28	Stk-R	80	44	.55	
	Jan 20	Mdn Clm	22	14	.63	
Imperious Spirit	Apr 6	Gr 1	100	28	.28	35
	Mar 19	Stk-R	80	34	.42	
	Mar 2	NWMC	45	28	.44	
	Feb 2	NWMC	45	31	.69	
	Jan 19	NWMC	45	14	.31	
Variety Road	Apr 6	Gr 1	100	28	.28	56
	Mar 16	Gr 1	100	48	.48	
	Feb 22	Gr 2	100	64	.64	
	Jan 29	Stk-R	80	48	.60	
	Jan 12	Stk-R	80	27	.34	
	Dec 29	Mdn	35	25	.71	
Jetting Home	Apr 6	Gr 1	100	28	.28	35
	Mar 12	Stk-0	80	36	.45	
	Feb 22	Gr 2	100	43	.43	
	Feb 2	NWMC	45	21	.44	
	Jan 9	NWMC	45	27	.60	
	Dec 27	NWMC	45	23	.51	

NOTE: Blueboy ratings that are underlined were used to obtain Blueboy ranks.
* Ranking must be considered tentative. Key races not rated.

The "most advanced" competitive level can be interpreted to refer not only to a specific level of the eligibility conditions but to strongly associated classes of races that regularly attract comparable horses. Maidens comprise a category apart, and the various conditions of eligibility can be grouped as follows:

Alw NWMC	Alw NW3xMC	Stk-L	Stk-Gr 2
Alw NW2xMC	Alw NW4xMC	Stk-Gr 3	Stk-Gr 1
	Clf Alw		
Stk-R	Stk-0		

Blueboy ranks can be considered standard scores that are interchangeable among racetracks and horse populations. They serve as well as percentiles. Percentiles are interpreted as rankings superior to all scores falling below, such that a rating of 80 is a percentile rank superior to 80 percent of the horses that have been rated.

By these techniques the leading horses in all divisions at the nation's racetracks can be ranked and compared reasonably well. Only the rare horses whose latest race and best race each received 100 percent of the class points would obtain a percentile ranking of 100. All percentile ranks can be referenced to the highest percentile rank of 100, whether real or hypothetical.

Ranks will change repeatedly as nonclaiming horses continue to develop their abilities and advance into stricter competition. For many horses below the division leaders, ultimate rankings may not stabilize until midway through the four-year-old season. They may begin to fall for just as many older horses soon after that. Class is relative, class is dynamic.

A practical problem associated with the method and local applications is dramatized by the unacceptably low ranking assigned to the Preakness winner Snow Chief, who annexed the Florida Derby as well while this study was in progress and the Jersey Derby later. The method cannot rate shippers unless par times, daily track variants, and CQ Scale ratings are available to evaluate races run at racetracks outside of the local circuit. Without the class ratings for the graded stakes it won at Bay Meadows and Gulfstream Park, Snow Chief cannot be evaluated properly and has been ranked here artificially, below its true percentile.

With long-distance shipping so commonplace among non-claiming horses nowadays, class handicappers will need par-time charts, result charts, and opportunities to watch the added-money races of all major tracks. If simulcasts are not available, result charts become mandatory, and in any case the unobserved races become seriously problematic for raters. A front-row view is more important than ever.

Putting the asterisk astride Snow Chief's ranking to indicate that the colt remains essentially unclassified, their Blueboy ranks allow handicappers to arrange the 1986 Santa Anita Derby starters in a line that corresponds well with real abilities:

Rank	Horse	Percentile
1	Ferdinand	64
2	Variety Road	56
3	Icy Groom	45
4	Snow Chief	37*
5	Big Play	37
6	Imperious Spirit	35
7	Jetting Home	35

Its percentile rank of 64 means Ferdinand has been judged superior to 64 percent of all thoroughbreds that have been or might be evaluated on class. An all-time great like Secretariat, who set track records unremittingly, if rated retroactively, would obtain a percentile rank of 100, and other greats such as Affirmed, Spectacular Bid, and Seattle Slew would be ranked close to the top.

Blueboy rankings permit hypothetical comparisons across generations as well as concrete distinctions among current division hopefuls. The method thereby facilitates unresolvable arguments about the history of events at the same time it does the making of money on the best horses today.